Soccer Drills for Kids Ages 8-12

By

Chest Dugger

Table Of Contents

About the Author

Chest Dugger is a soccer fan, former professional and coach now looking to share his knowledge. Enjoy this book and several others that he has written.

Free Gift Included

As part of our dedication to help you succeed in your career, we have sent you a free soccer drills worksheet, known as the "Soccer Training Work Sheet" drill sheet. The worksheet is a list of drills that you can use to improve your game and a methodology to track your performance on these drills on a day-to-day basis. We want to get you to the next level.

Click on the link below to get your free drills worksheet.

https://soccertrainingabiprod.gr8.com/

Disclaimer

Introduction – The Best Age to Coach

A call from Barcelona apart, the opportunity to coach a group of boys or girls (or, increasingly, both) in the eight to twelve age range is the most exciting challenge an amateur coach can enjoy. Coaching kids is always rewarding. There's the pleasure of spending time doing something we love, the chance to test our own soccer knowledge and motivational skills in the pressure pot of a match, the challenge of putting together a programme to turn our team into one that is as good as it can be. All of that is still there, but added to this glorious recipe comes the satisfaction of knowing we are helping children to progress, to develop. Not just in their soccer or even sporting endeavours, but in all aspects of their lives.

Team sports can offer crucial life skills which help young people to cope better with the challenges the slings and arrows of unexpected fortune throws at them, to make friendships, to develop mental strength and resilience. Suddenly, we play a part in the development of those children. While doing something we love. How good is that?

And here's the rub, we are doing it with the best age group to coach. This is not to decry the importance of coaching very young children, or for that matter teenagers. Anybody who works in youth activities – professionally or, as mostly in our case, as a keen amateur, is making a significant contribution to our society. A vitally important one at that. In many ways, the most important one. We are helping to turn a set of young people into the adults we would all hope they become. But…and there are a couple of these…working with five or six year olds is not easy. We are less a coach and need to be more a child development specialist. Some people are great with this age, have the patience of a coach at Tottenham Hotspur FC and the calmness of the best of referees. Nor is running an under fifteen side always a stride alongside the shrubbery. Although, helping this age group is also to fulfil a very important role. Here, we are helping to keep a group of teenagers to keep off the streets, we are utilising their enthusiasm for sport to give them a purpose outside of school and home. We are working to focus their rebellious natures onto something positive. It's all hugely worthwhile, and if we have to put up with the occasional (or more frequent) surliness, cockiness and conflict of hormones as boys and girls discover that the opposite sex can be more than just an annoyance, well, that's the price we pay for our altruism.

But eight to twelve year old kids are the best age to coach. These are kids who have already developed a high level of coordination.

7

There's still a way for them to go, especially at the lower levels of this range, but these are children in control of their limbs. They are also old enough to have a reasonably good level of concentration so drills can be explained, and tactics introduced. They are old enough to have chosen for themselves to play soccer at our club, and to understand what this commitment involves. So their enthusiasm is still there, but their expectations are realistic. At the same time, they are young enough to listen to what we say; their questions will be genuine and their thirst for learning at its height.

Our philosophy in this book of drills and skills is simple. We believe that soccer is a great game, the best game in the world. It helps to keep us fit, it teaches us the importance of teamwork, of friendship and of loyalty to our peers. It introduces us to different people from different backgrounds and thankfully is becoming ever more inclusive. Although there is still a way to go in this area at the elite level, clubs are now welcoming to people from all genders, backgrounds and ethnicity. Soccer teaches us mental acuity and emotional strength and makes us more resilient in our everyday lives.

With young people our focus is on our skills and technique, on teamwork and on fun. We believe it is great to win, and there is nothing wrong with that, but it is also important to learn how to lose well and respect our opponents whether they beat us, or we them. We believe that competition is important and is a part of both growing up and living in the adult world. But this competition must remain enjoyable, and as soon as winning becomes more important than taking part we are starting to go wrong. The old cliché still holds as much relevance as it ever did. It's not the winning, it's the taking part.

Mostly, though, we believe that our players are at the heart of what we do. Everything we coach is for them, and the most talented potential future pro is as important as the young lad who struggles to pass a ball accurately more than five metres. In fact, the future pro is the most important person in our coaching world. Except, it is a position he or she shares, no more nor less, with the kid who is struggling but who still wants to be the best that they can. If we hold that thought at the forefront of our thinking, then we won't be going too far wrong.

Each of our chapters focusses on a specific element of soccer pertinent to the eight to twelve age range. Our youngest players are therefore likely to be just eight, our eldest twelve. These are quite different beasts in terms of coordination and spatial awareness, in terms of concentration and motor skills and in terms of their ability to use technique to learn new skills. So depending on the age group we are coaching, we need to be selective in the drills we choose, and prepared to adapt and develop them to suit the needs of our players.

Many of the following fifty drills, activities and tips (along with techniques, tactics and games) include diagrams. They have been used to help with clarity in understanding the operation of the exercises. In these, the following symbols are used:

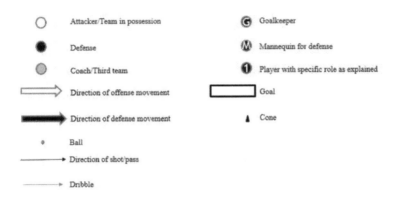

There are specific explanations of symbols by some drills, and they are not drawn to scale.

The drills are designed to be fun for the players, whilst also developing necessary skills for playing the game. Our drills are made up of teamwork activities, mental health exercises for players and other drills specific to certain skills. However, they are best used as starters for coaches to adapt to their own group and to fit with their own resources of equipment and staffing. In that sense, the potential is there for soccer-inspiring aids for coaches, managers and trainers. Or indeed anyone with an interest in instilling a love of soccer in eight to twelve year olds.

Spatial Awareness

Spatial awareness is a term we hear used a lot. Maybe not always with a firm grasp of what it actually means. A toddler crashes into a table; 'they're learning about spatial awareness', a youngster gets too close to another when lining up for their lunch, 'he's not got much of a sense of spatial awareness'. A footballer trips over the ball. 'Where's their spatial awareness?'

So what exactly does the term mean? Each of the above are reasonable examples, spatial awareness is our ability to interact with our environment. To be aware of our own position in relation to that of other people and objects, and to understand the body control required to perform a particular task. For example, innately calculating how far an arm must extend to deflect a shot around the post. Although, to be precise, this definition actually describes a process called proprioception, but spatial awareness works well enough for our purposes. The process is instinctive yet at the same time improves with practice and experience.

Spatial awareness is something young children are developing. By the time they reach our under-eight side they are pretty good at it. Amazing, in fact, given they have only been able to get up on their legs for a few years. There are a number of factors, though, about which we need to be aware because they inhibit children's abilities to develop spatial awareness. Surprisingly, perhaps, it is a cognitive rather than physical skill, and sadly some kids find it a really difficult one to acquire. Among the conditions which can inhibit a child's ability to have good spatial awareness are autism spectrum disorder, or ASD, dyspraxia and ADHD. We know that these are common disorders among young people. As schools, parents and medical professionals become better at identifying children with a specific challenge which inhibits their ability to use spatial awareness, so the numbers identified increase. Injury to the right side of the brain can also halt or slow a person's ability to develop the cognitive function required for good spatial awareness.

Imagine how hard that must be. We are growing up and becoming aware that we somehow do not see the world as other people do; we find it impossible to read social signals which are as clear as day to other people, so we are constantly criticised or rebuffed because we do something that seems fine to us, but is rejected by our friends and peers. Now all we want to do is be able to kick a soccer ball like we see our heroes do on TV, or our friends in the playground. But we can't. Our

13

brains simply do not calculate the amount of force needed to pass a ball to a team mate, or the angle our foot needs to be to complete this task. Something which seems so simple to everybody else.

In the old days we used to have a couple of terms for children such as this. We called them uncoordinated or clumsy. A little further back we used even less pleasant terms, which we certainly will not repeat here. These days, thank goodness, our understanding is a lot better. We cannot make a child with spatial awareness problems overcome their difficulties by waving the magic wand of soccer, but we can certainly help. For us coaches, that is a big responsibility to hold.

Of course, we are not that likely to come across too many children with big problems in this field, especially if we coach towards the upper end of our age range. Very sadly such children have probably already decided that soccer is not for them. Another field in which they can gain little success. But all young people are learning to improve their sense of spatial awareness, and even where it is very highly developed, it can get better still. The drills which follow will help our young players become more aware of the environment in which they play the game, and indeed all of the drills and techniques we cover in this book will help young people with motor control and awareness of space and their position within it.

It is a truth that when we coach young people to play our beautiful game, we are not only helping them to develop good lifestyle habits, friendships, mental strength and social skills, but awareness of their place in their environment, and the motor control required to maximise the benefits of that place. This is a truth that permeates every chapter of this book, although we will not repeat it in each section.

Drill: Simple Warm Up

This is a useful drill to employ during a warm up, as it is very simple to learn and involves lots of players in activity.

Use With: Any age.

Objectives: Dribble with the ball under control whilst being aware of cross passes. Pass across the grid with awareness of dribblers.

Equipment: Grid 20 metres by 20 metres. Balls.

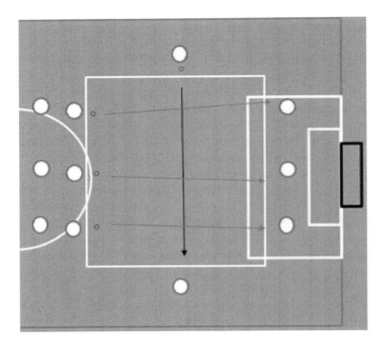

Operation of Drill: The drill as explained here involves eleven players but can be used with more or less. Line up three players evenly spaced on one side of the grid. Each has a ball. Three further players line up behind them, and on the opposite side of the grid are three more. About half way across the grid are two players on opposite sides, who also have one ball.

The three players at the end dribble across the grid before laying off the ball to their three team mates opposite. These then dribble back and so on. Meanwhile the two players across the grid pass backwards

16

and forwards. These two players must pass regularly, with one, two or three touches depending on ability level, but must also be aware of the dribblers. All players work as quickly as they can, but maintain awareness of the dribblers.

Change the passers regularly.

Key Skills:

- Dribbling using the laces to propel the ball.
- Remain close to the ball so that the passes across the pitch can be avoided.
- Change pace and direction to avoid passes.
- Pass firmly using the instep.
- Pass with awareness of the dribblers.
- Receive the ball with the shoulder advanced towards the ball, on the half turn that is. This both develops this skill and allows the receiver to shift the ball to create an angle to avoid the dribbling players.

Development:

- Add an extra pair of passers.

17

Drill: Escaped Convicts

This is lively, energetic activity similar to the traditional fun game of Pirates. It is one which helps to develop spatial awareness whilst at the same time providing lots of movement and changes of direction. It can be played indoors if the facility exists, using gym mats as the 'safe' spaces.

Use With: Because it does not involve a ball until the end, the coordination required is less than in similar sorts of drills, so it works well with younger children. However, older ones within our age range will love the chasing element as well. It is basically a tag game, and works effectively as a warmup, or as something to provide variety amongst other more static drills.

A word of warning – it takes a while to create the environment for this drill so either do so in advance, or get a helper to prepare the activity whilst the group are working on something else. There is no hard and fast rules as to how the activity needs to be set up. However, keep safety at the forefront of planning as there will be a lot of movement and action in the drill.

18

Objectives: Work as a team to escape from captivity. In order to make their 'escape', convicts must pass through the various hazards without being tagged, and then score a goal.

Equipment: Lots. Balls for 'escape'. These are placed within shooting distance of the goal. Bibs, three colours required.

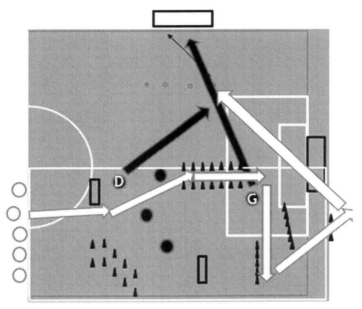

(Note: the diagram shows a much less busy grid than anticipated, and limited movement from players. This is because the diagram can quickly become even more confusing. The idea of the drill is that everybody is moving and it is a couple of minutes of (not very) organised chaos. With all the fun that entails!)

19

Operation of Drill: Divide the group into two. One group are 'convicts', the other guards. The aim is for as many convicts to escape (by passing through the various hazards without being caught, and then scoring a goal) as possible. The guards wear bibs. One wears a different colour, and he or she is the goalkeeper, who may move to the goal to save shots and stop the convicts escaping. Another wears a third colour of bib. This is the defender, who may attempt to tackle the convicts when they try to 'scale the wall' by scoring a goal.

Set up a grid using half a pitch and covering about one half of the width of the pitch. Set up a goal on the opposite touch line, and place a number of balls around twenty metres from the goal.

In the grid are a number of obstacles, such as mannequins or small portable goals. Set up 'walls' of cones which cannot be crossed by any player etc. Set up some 'tunnels'. At the opposite end to the start line set up a gate through which the convicts must escape.

The 'tunnels' are safe areas for the convicts, and the guards cannot enter these.

The convicts start at one end. They have two minutes to escape. They escape by getting through the escape gate, then passing to the shooting area and scoring. If they score, they escape. If they are tagged in the grid area, or they do not score (shot saved, tackled or shot off target), they must go back to the start line.

Each convict who escapes counts as one point. At the end of the two minutes, swap bibs and change roles. Then the other team tries to escape. The game can be run three or four times to see who gets the best overall tally.

This is a complicated game, although coaches will adapt it to their own needs. However, for clarity, the above instructions are repeated below in bullet point format.

- Divide into two groups – convicts and guards.
- Guards wear bibs. There are fewer guards than convicts.
- There are two goals at 90 degrees to each other.
- One guard wears a different coloured bib. This is the goalkeeper who is permitted to move to the goal when they wish.
- Another guard wears a third colour of bib. This is the defender who may move to the goal area when a convict reaches a ball. They may then try to tackle the convict before they score.

21

- Guards aim to 'tag' the convicts.

- Convicts start on the start line.

- They must pass through a gate opposite.

- There are various obstacles they must avoid.

- There are also tunnels made of cones. These are safe areas for convicts to 'hide' in. Guards are not permitted in the tunnels.

- Convicts escape by completing the following two stages:
  - Pass through the gate without being tagged.
  - Then sprint to a ball and score a goal.

- If convicts are tagged before passing through the gate, or do not score a goal, they return to the start line and try again.

- Convicts have two minutes in which to escape.

Key Skills:

- Communication with team mates. For example, it is easy to become trapped in a tunnel, so work as a team to escape. Similarly, once through the gate, a player is safe from being tagged, so can wait for some team mates to attack the goal simultaneously, increasing the chance of scoring.

22

Development:

- Introduce other 'escape' skills, such as ten juggles, or chip over a wall, to fit with other skills being developed in the session.

Drill: The Goal Doesn't Move

Many years ago, before he became better known for defeating the British Government and the BBC with his Twitter activities, the England Striker Gary Lineker tormented First Division and international defences with his goal threat. Once, after a particularly impressive performance, he was asked by a sports presenter how he knew where to shoot when he had his back to goal. 'Well, the goal doesn't move,' he replied with a smile.

Mr Lineker is of course right. But that does not mean that young players are always clear as to where their target is located. The following drill helps to develop that awareness through practice, and using markers to help orientate themselves.

Use With: This is a fairly high skill level drill, and while it is ideal for older players in the 8-12 age range, younger ones may struggle with the coordination of the turn.

Objectives: With the back to goal, control and turn under pressure and shoot on target, aiming for the far post.

Equipment: Balls. Mannequins as stationary defenders, although real defenders can be used. Goal, goalkeeper, and feeders.

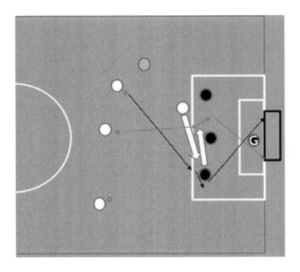

(Note, in the diagram above the thin black lines represent the first set of pass, touch, shoot, the lighter grey lines the second set.)

Operation of Drill: The drill involves eight players, or five if mannequins are used. Set up three defenders (mannequins) across the width of the goal, positioned just inside the penalty area. The striker is a metre in front of this line. There are three feeders, and the coach indicates from whom a pass will be made (or a leader can be appointed to decide this). The striker runs in front of a defender. The striker can choose which of these he attacks, as long as he varies his position. Movement is crucial to finding the space needed to get away a shot. He gets on the half turn to receive the pass, controls the ball, swivels and shoots, aiming for the far post. He or she then immediately sprints in front of a new defender to receive another pass. Give each striker six shots then change positions.

Key Skills:

- First touch on the half turn to take the ball out of the striker's feet and allow the swivel and shot.
- Strike cleanly with the laces for power, or instep for accuracy or curl.
- Aim for the far post (either post when the shot is central).
- Be on the move all the time.
- Use indicators on the pitch – lines, bags of balls, whatever there is, to help orientate the position. (Note, once using

this drill a good player kept shooting wide, after hitting the target a couple of times to begin with. Asked why, the lad said that he was using a marker to help him locate the posts. Unfortunately, it turned out he had selected a leaf on the pitch, which had moved a few yards after a gust of wind. Ensure players pick something that won't suffer the same fate!)

Development:

- If using real defenders, allow them to move and pressure the ball.

Drill: Dribble Zones

This is a handy drill which works well as a warm up in addition to developing both spatial awareness and dribbling skills.

Use With: Any age.

Objectives: Dribble between different shaped zones, being aware of team mates' movements.

Equipment: Four grids, balls.

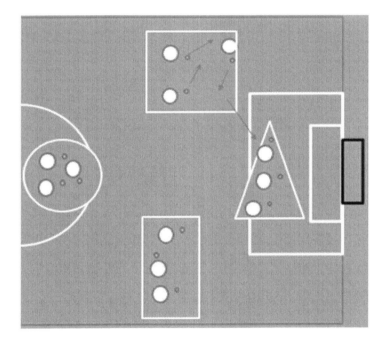

Operation of Drill: Set up four differently shaped grids as per the diagram. Players divide themselves equally between the four grids. This is also the maximum number allowed in any grid at one time. Players

27

dribble within the grid for fifteen to twenty seconds, without making any contact with another player. The coach blows their whistle and the players dribble to any other grid. However, they must be aware of their teammates' movement to ensure the maximum number in any grid is not passed. They dribble for fifteen to twenty seconds in the new grid, and so on. Repeat five to six times. Pause to get feedback on challenges and techniques, then repeat.

Key Skills:

- Dribbling under close control.
- Awareness of the movement of team mates.
- Decision making.

Development: Add defenders between the zones who must try to make a tackle whilst players are moving between the grids.

By working with drills such as these, we will help to speed up a player's developing sense of space around them. It is a natural process for most, but we can help it along.

Passing Drills

What constitutes a good pass in soccer? That is something we probably know instinctively, yet it is harder to define, or to break down into its constituent elements. But if we are to teach young players how to become good passers of the ball, then we must ensure they understand what constitutes a good pass, and what a bad one looks like. These characteristics permeate any drills which focus on the skill of passing, and a good coach reiterates them regularly, both to the group and to individual players.

The first, and perhaps most obvious, characteristic is accuracy. Again, we can define what an accurate pass looks like. Because this does vary depending on the position of the receiver, the location of opponents, and the purpose of the pass. Sometimes, a delivery will aim to inject pace into an attack, launching a counter offensive. At other times, it will be played for tactical advantage, say when seeking to switch play and move the opponent's defense around. Occasionally a pass deliberately slows play, to allow team mates to recover their positions. So the concept of accuracy is a moveable feast. Within that definition, however, we can apply a couple of broad rules to instil into our young charges. For a player *standing still*, or *running towards the ball carrier* a pass should ideally be to feet. This gives maximum opportunity to bring the ball under control, and protect it from any opponents.

However, *for a player running forwards, even at an angle*, the ideal pass is played in front of them so they can receive the ball without breaking stride. This ensures pace in the move is not lost. Of course, the position of the nearest defender determines how far in front of the receiver the pass is played.

The second characteristic of the best pass is its pace. The speed of the pass takes into account the movement and skill level of the receiver. For example, *a player running towards the ball* needs a slightly softer pass, or the combined speed of the ball allied to the opposite direction in which the receiver is running will mean control is difficult. A ball hit in front of a team mate needs to be weighted so that the *player takes control without needing to change direction or speed*.

The next crucial element is timing. This is something much harder to define and is almost instinctive. Although, as any coach knows, instinct improves with practice! The best passers read the movements of both their team mates and their opponents. They pick the moment an opponent cannot intercept, because they are too far away, or focussed on another defensive role such as guarding space or marking an opponent. They read the run a team mate will make, and whether they are expecting a pass. We can encourage our young players to watch professional football and absorb the ways in which the best passers time their delivery so well.

Great passers 'see' the killer ball. (We are not sure that this perception can be taught, but the innate presence of it exists in every player to a greater or lesser extent. As coaches, through drills, encouragement, and good advice we can help a player to fulfil the potential they possess in this field). Great passers read the development of play and become aware of how spaces develop. They are able to fool opponents by striking the ball early or late, using different parts of their foot or deceiving a defender with their eyes. However, there is one element which is perhaps more important than any other, because without it they will never get the opportunity to play the pass. That is the ability to have a good first touch. This means protecting the ball on receipt of it, cushioning just away from the feet and ideally receiving on the half turn. This technique requires receipt of the ball in a position between being square to it (chest facing) and sideways (shoulder facing). The body is half turned, which means either foot can control the ball, and the first touch can allow the ball to be protected, turned forwards to launch an attack or backwards to protect possession.

31

A good first touch gives the player time to find and play their pass, and given time, most of us become closer to an Iniesta, and less of a 1930s centre half.

Drill: Warm Up Rondo

Go to see a leading professional team and during the pre-match warm up, the following type of passing rondo will be in use. If it is good enough for a top players, then it is good enough for us. The drill is really simple and is an excellent way to start a session. One problem with which coaches will be familiar is that sessions with children sometimes get off to a bad start because the coach is engaged with parents, answering questions and so forth, and the players have little to do. They then descend into taking corners, or shooting, and only a few are involved while others become bored. It means a chaotic start to a session, and as every teacher knows, start a lesson badly and it rarely improves.

However, we can tell our players that every session begins with the following drill. One which requires nothing beyond a ball, and can be organised by the team themselves. Even the youngest soccer players will understand what is required here. At the same time, the drill is encouraging good technique by ensuring players are in the right position to receive the ball and lay it off quickly.

Use With: All age groups.

Objectives: Keep possession of the ball against limited opposition.

Equipment: Balls.

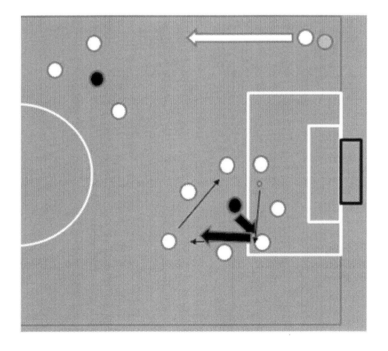

Operation of Drill: Players join the activity as they arrive for the session. They form a broad circle about eight to ten metres in diameter and pass the ball across this area. One player is in the middle and must intercept the ball. When successful, this player swaps with the one who has just lost possession.

As the group grows less movement is needed. Make sure a particular collection of players does not get too large. Set the limit at around seven or eight participants and once the next arrival goes to join their mates, three break off to join the newcomer and start a second group working on this rondo passing drill.

Key Skills:

- Communication with eyes, gestures and words as to where the ball will be passed.
- On toes to receive the ball, shoulder facing on the half turn.
- One touch to control away from the opposition, second touch to pass.
- Pass smoothly with the instep.

Development:

- With strong groups, make the circle smaller, which requires a better first touch and increases pressure.

Drill: Through the Gate

One of our favourite drills for passing features three sets of five players who pass from end to end of a long grid, trying to evade the team based in the centre who must intercept the deliveries being made. It is a great drill, but appears in other books and is also quite complicated, and maybe a little too difficult for most under tens and below. Here is an adaptation of the drill which builds on many of the same skills, but requires less of a requirement to strike the ball hard over a longish distance, and is therefore more appropriate for our age range.

Use With: All within the age range, although it might not present enough challenge to the most able under twelves..

Objectives: Pass the ball accurately along the ground from one end of a grid to the other.

35

Equipment: Balls, grid, cones, bibs.

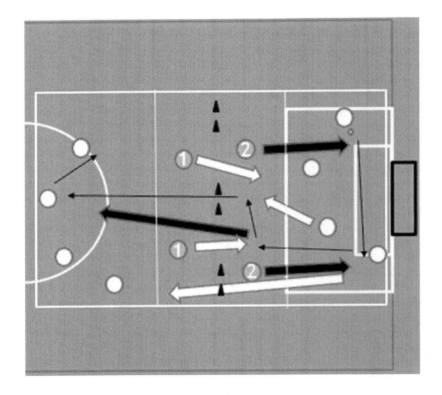

Operation of Drill: The drill is played on a thirty-metre-long grid, which is twenty metres wide. It is divided into three equal portions. In the middle portion are three 'gates' through which the ball must be passed. Twelve players are divided into three teams of four, with four of the players based in the centre who change roles depending on the location of the ball.

36

There are four players at either end, who play together to pass the ball through the central gates. The middle team are divided into two pairs, wearing different coloured bibs. One pair become helpers to the team in possession (Number 1 in grey on the diagram). They must stay in the middle zone, and feed passes to the team in possession, so they can pass through the gate to the other end. The other pair are defenders (Number 2). They must go into the end zone of the team in possession and try to win the ball. Meanwhile, the team without the ball, that is, the team at the opposite end to

the ball, move to position themselves to receive the pass through the gate when it comes.

The team in possession must create space for a pass to one of their temporary team mates in the centre zone. They put a pass into this zone. One of their team can then move into the middle zone to receive a return pass and knock the ball through the gate and into the other end of the pitch.

Each successful pass through a gate and into the other end zone scores a point. If the ball goes out of play, the defenders win the ball or it is passed missing the gate, no points are scored and play restarts with the receivers taking possession.

37

After the pass is played the following happens.

1) The team at the other end now become the team in possession.
2) The team who have just played the pass retreat to or remain in their end zone, ready for the next pass.
3) The two players who have just been defenders move back into the middle zone, and now become the additional attackers for the new team in possession.
4) The two players who have just supported the team in attack move into the opposite end zone and become defenders.

Play for three minutes then swap groups. Tally up the points scored by each team. The team in the middle must perform their roles to the best of their ability. They are keen, enthusiastic players, so they will.

Key Skills:

- Teamwork to create space for the pass into the middle zone.
- Technique to pass firmly, with the instep, through a gate and to the other end of the pitch.

- Receiving the ball on the half turn (such a vital skill, the younger it is learned, the better) and first touch to give the player in possession options for the next pass.
- Pressuring as defenders and working together to stop an attack.

Development:

- Introduce one or two touch passing in the centre zone.
- This both injects pace, and is therefore realistic to the match situation, and also requires top technique to retain control of the ball.

Drill: The Switch

One of the challenges facing coaches of younger age groups is the honeypot effect. This is where players migrate to the ball, and space is denied to all. Learning how to play the switch early helps to prevent this difficulty from setting in, and also helps young players to understand about space, and the importance of finding it. Sometimes, younger players feel that they are not involved unless directly playing the ball.

However, the switch teaches them that positional sense is important, and then when they do get the ball, they often have the space they require to use it effectively.

Use With: All age ranges. It may be necessary to narrow the width of the pitch where younger players struggle to kick the ball over a large distance. However, it is the principle of the technique on which we focus with this drill, so it is still good to use it with even Under Eights.

Objectives: Switch the play to create a goal scoring chance.

Equipment: Balls. Goal.

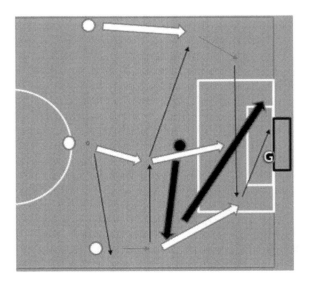

Operation of Drill: Three attackers, one defender and a goalkeeper. Rotate positions after each run. The drill begins with the player in the centre. The defender is opposite him or her, with team mates on either side.

The player in possession passes to either team mate. They control the ball and run on to draw the defender. When the defender is committed, they pass square in front of the original player. This player now places a first time pass in front of the other team mate. He waits for the defender to be drawn over then pulls the ball back for either of the other team mates to shoot and score.

Key Skills:

- Pass accurately and firmly along the ground to maximise the likelihood of keeping possession.
- Pass using the instep, head over the ball and striking firmly.
- Pass in front of the team mate so they can run onto the ball.
- Pass first time where necessary.
- Shoot first time with accuracy.

41

Development:

- Encourage use of the skill by shouting 'Switch' when appropriate during a small sided game
- Reward attempts at the switch to encourage players to take the decision to use the switch in match situations themselves
- Similarly, reward players who hold their position wide when their side is in possession.
- Alternatively, miss out the central player to make the switch with one longer pass. A much harder skill which requires longer kicking distance, accuracy over a greater distance and better control from the receiver, as such a pass is likely to be played in the air.

Drill: Pass and Move

A simple but effective little drill to get players into the habit of moving after their pass. It is easy to set up, and active for our players.

Use With: Any age.

Objectives: Pass and receive with good technique, move after the pass.

Equipment: Four cones, two balls.

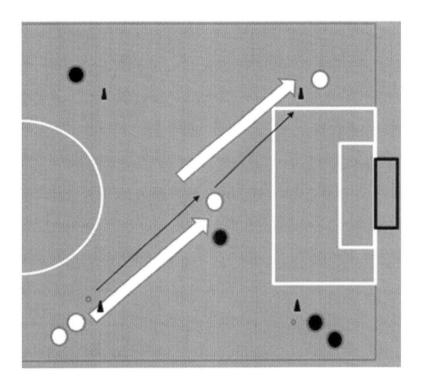

Operation of Drill: The drill requires eight players but will also work with four or twelve. With four participants, divide into two pairs, with twelve into four groups of three. When working the drill with eight players divide them into four groups of two. Each pair starts by a cone. Two of the pairs who are on adjacent corners begin with a ball. The ball

43

is passed into the middle. A player from each of the opposite sides moves into the middle to receive the pass, turns 180 degrees and passes to the opposite corner. Players follow their passes. The players in the middle go to the back of the line to which they are running.

Key Skills:

- Pass with side foot, firmly along the ground.
- Follow the pass.
- Receive the pass on the half turn, using either foot.
- Control to allow a 180 degree turn.

Development: Remove one ball and allow the player in the middle to pass to any of the corners. Here the player must play their first touch to allow them to pass to their target with their second touch. A defender can be added in the centre to add more pressure to the player.

A game of soccer is a piece of drama. The passes are the plot lines, the beautiful creations which help shape the story. A drama also needs pace and energy, something to drive the audience towards the denouement, which is, for soccer, a goal. There is no better way to engage the crowd's passion than with what will be the focus of our next chapter.

A Short message from the Author:

Hey, are you enjoying the book? I'd love to hear your thoughts!

Many readers do not know how hard reviews are to come by, and how much they help an author.

I would be incredibly thankful if you could take just 60 seconds to write a brief review on Amazon, even if it's just a few sentences!

Browse to the product page and leave a review as shown below.

Thank you for taking the time to share your thoughts!

Your review will genuinely make a difference for me and help gain exposure for my work.

Dribbling

A great shot, a crunching tackle, a superb save. Each serves to get the crowd to its feet. They are what makes soccer the world's greatest sport. But in order to get those moments of explosive drama we need anticipation. Nothing teases that anticipation like a thrilling dribble. There is something magical about watching Messi weave through the eyes of needles, ball glued to his feet, or Vinicius Jr streaking down the wing leaving the full back flailing in his wake. Seeing Beth Mead or Lauren Kelly roar past defenders. The crowd just knows that something special is going to happen. We just know it.

As with other skills in soccer, there are several elements to be found in a good dribbler. Pace is clearly one. Although we can help a young player to run faster by helping them to develop technique and promote explosive muscle control, we cannot turn a steam roller into a Ferrari. Yet that is not the problem. The biggest inhibitor to pace for a soccer player is ball control. If the player is constantly having to slow to make a touch on the ball, even a half a million-dollar supercar can be tamed by the Ford Fiesta seeking to outpace it. Watch clips of Maradona, Thierry Henry or Cristiano Ronaldo in their prime though, and we can see these powerful sports cars driven to their best. These players never break stride to propel the ball, it is as though it has become an extendable limb, completely under their control. And that technique is something we can teach.

Even without explosive pace, a dribbler can be effective. They can learn the tricks of dribbling; the feint, the step over, the directional change created by such as the Cruyff turn or the hook turn. Finally a good dribbler can create space for others by knowing where to run, whether to cut inside taking their marker with them thus creating space outside of them or whether to accelerate wide, and when to lay off the pass for maximum effect.

Drill Nine: Various Dribbles

One of the key elements of coaching children of this age is to keep sessions active. There's a well-known saying which comes from ancient China that perfectly encapsulates the philosophy here. It is not original, or even that unusual, but is perfect to keep at the forefront of our thinking when we are planning sessions. Roughly translated, the saying goes:

'I hear and I forget.

I see and I remember.

I do and I understand.'

Put simply, as coaches we talk less and get the children doing more. The recipe for a successful coaching session. This drill is so simple and so active that it fits this methodology like a well-loved soccer boot on a slightly aching foot. Comfortable yet effective.

Use With: All ages.

Objectives: Dribble under control, shoot across the goal to score.

Equipment: Balls, cones.

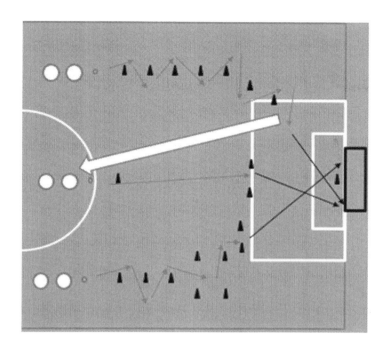

Operation of Drill: Divide the group into three. Set up three dribbling zones to fit the skills you wish to hone. In the diagram we have one close dribbling run, one running with the ball run and one lane which includes a step over, change of direction and then a shot. The players simply complete the run, shoot into the opposite corner, collect their ball and join the next run. Once the drill begins it takes a life of its own and the children are in virtually continuous action. As coach, the only organisation needed is to slow down a runner if the person in front loses control of the ball. Otherwise, we can concentrate on encouragement and coaching points.

49

Key Skills:

- Use both feet to dribble, keeping the ball close ready to beat an opponent.
- Run with the ball using the laces and avoid breaking stride.
- Step over:
  - Lift one foot over the ball and plant beside it;
  - Drop the opposite shoulder;
  - Use the outside of the other foot to shift the ball in the opposite direction;
  - Accelerate away with the ball.
- Shoot with instep.
  - Use arms for balance;
  - Lean slightly away when aiming for the opposite corner;
  - The ball should curl inwards if using the inside foot, outwards if using the outermost foot. Allow for this curl with the shot.

Development:

- Add alternative dribbling tasks, such as combined close dribbling, running with the ball or runs with a change of pace zone.

Drill: Beating the Last Defender

We want our players to be able to think for themselves. In many ways our job as coach is to arm them with a variety of skills and good technique, then let them free to learn what works and what does not. We all learn from failure, provided we see this as something that provides positive opportunities rather than a negative experience. Children are no exception.

To get the most out of this drill it helps to have assistants on hand, and therefore we can work with relatively small groups of three or four players and offer them immediate and valid coaching tips. Keep feedback short; say what goes well in any run, and perhaps suggest other techniques a player could use to beat the defender. These might include change of pace, step over (if the player is able, even multiple step overs), Cruyff or hook turn, dropping the shoulder and so forth.)

51

Use With: All players.

Objectives: Beat the last defender and get a shot off.

Equipment: Balls, mannequin.

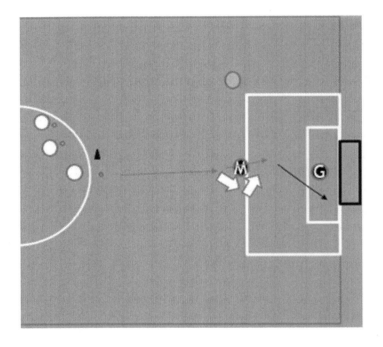

Operation of Drill: Work, if possible, with multiple small groups, each with a goal, goalkeeper, mannequin and three to four players trying out the drill. It is very simple. Players take it in turns to begin at the cone. They dribble towards the mannequin located around the edge of the box. They use a piece of skill of their own choosing to beat the mannequin. They then shoot to score.

Key Skills:

- Try a variety of techniques to beat the defender.
- Once space is created, shoot early and aim for the corners.

Development:

- Replace the mannequin with an active defender.

Drill: One v One

This drill gives players an opportunity to try out various skills in a semi competitive environment. It works well as both a warm up and a drill in its own right.

Use With: All ages.

Objectives: Dribble through gates using a variety of skills to beat a partner.

Equipment: Balls, Cones.

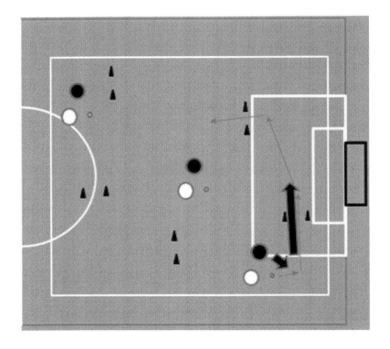

Operation of Drill: This is a simple drill which helps with fitness, defending and, most importantly for this chapter, dribbling skills. Set up a large grid, the size to be determined by the number of players involved. Using a penalty area or a half pitch can save time laying out the grid. As always, the stronger and more skilful the players, the smaller the area to be used. Inside the grid lay out a random set of gates. Players pair up, one is the dribbler and the other is the defender. Run the drill for thirty seconds to a minute, depending on the age of the players. Thirty seconds does not sound long but it is a fair time to be constantly moving at speed. The dribbler must dribble through as many gates as possible within the time limit, his partner attempting to stop him (within the laws of the game!). It is fine to pass through a gate, do a Cruyff turn, and go back through the same gate from the other direction. If a tackle is made, the ball is played back to the attacker. Each gate passed through equates to one point. Have a short rest between time periods, then reverse roles and continue.

Key Skills:

- Use a variety of dribbling skills to beat a player and pass through a gate.
- Defend by shepherding dribblers away from the gates and onto their weaker foot.

Development:

- Make the area smaller.

Drill: Round the Keeper

This is a fun drill which children love to play. It is simple to set up, and involves dribblers accelerating towards the keeper, beating them with a bit of skill, and scoring into the empty net. Allow players to shoot as well, rather than rounding the keeper, but insist that they use a piece of skill such as a feint or step over to trick the keeper and create the space for the shot.

Use With: Any age. With the smaller goal option, players will need to be more able as scoring is much more difficult and will usually require the keeper to be rounded.

Objectives: Dribble at a keeper and score a goal.

Equipment: Goals and balls.

56

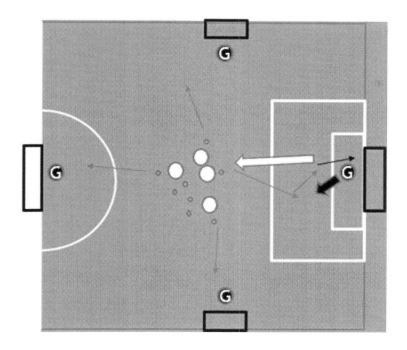

Operation of Drill: It could not be more straight forward. Simply the striker dribbles at the keeper, attempts to round them or draw them out of position, and tries to score. In order to involve more players, various smaller goals can be set up around the pitch to allow more variety.

Here, once the attempt has been made, the player retrieves their ball and dribbles to the next goal as per the diagram. Now there are four or more players attempting the drill at the same time. With different sized goals, the skill level required varies at each attempt.

Key Skills:

- Run with the ball at pace.

- Use a skill to deceive the keeper.

- Shoot accurately into the net.

- Encourage players to attempt a variety of skills.

- At the same time, try to get players to develop a trademark skill, one at which they will become extremely adept. In practical terms this might involve using the trademark skill, for example a step over and feint, fifty per cent of the time, while experimenting with other skills for the remainder of the time.

- The drill also provides good practice for the goalkeepers. They should:
    - Advance to narrow the angle;
    - Stay low and wide, but not go to ground until the player either shoots or attempts to round them;
    - Remain as large as possible;
    - Adopt the star shape if facing a shot. Here both arms spread wide, the body drops and the supporting leg faces parallel to the goal, stretch with knee bent, whilst the other leg stretches out straight in the opposite direction.

o If the dribbler attempts to round the keeper, they should wait until the attacker knocks the ball wider in order to beat them, and at that point attempt to deflect the ball, or gather it. Timing is all, but the onus is on the striker to score, as the majority of the time they should.

Development:

- Add a defender, starting a little way behind the dribbler. Here the defender attempts to catch up and make a tackle, or force the player to shoot earlier than wished. At the same time, if the striker dribbles across the defender it is harder to tackle them because of the risk of giving away a penalty or receiving a red card for making a foul as the last defender and denying a goal scoring opportunity. Of course, rarely are red cards issued at the level we are discussing in this book, but it is good to get into the best habits early!
- Set a time limit in which players can score.
- Each of these developments adds a time pressure to the dribbler.

The excitement grows! We have covered passing and dribbling in the last two chapters, and now it is time to move onto the element of soccer which is integral to the purpose of the game. Scoring goals, that is.

Shooting

'If you don't shoot, you can't score.' Never has a cliché held more truth. But we have all seen it, even at the very highest level of the professional game. A player is in the perfect position to shoot…and passes. The defense covers and the chance is lost. The collective sigh from the crowd is piteous to hear. Sixty thousand people let down in an instant. We scream 'Shoot' at the TV, or from our position in the stands, but the player has chosen not to. Most probably, because in the fraction of a second that offered the opportunity, a minute doubt enters the player's mind. It is enough in a sport requiring split second decisions. Hesitate. The chance is gone.

Our under nines might not quite operate in the same pressure cooker atmosphere, but there is an important lesson here for coaches of young players. We must encourage them to shoot, and reward them when they do. Praise for having a go. We can caveat that praise by asking about what alternatives they had, but only when we can see that the shot is ill judged. But our job is to build their confidence, and we do that through encouragement and not criticism. Equally, we ensure team mates also encourage the player rather than let them know that they were in a much better position and should have been fed the pass. We are all in a better position when a shot comes in and misses!

It's a strange thing. When a goalie dives, he or she will save the ball more often than not. Or their movement will force the striker to shoot wide or over. If they were to only save one shot in ten, then we would probably be politely looking for a new keeper. When a player makes a pass, sixty, seventy or eighty per cent of the time that pass will find a teammate. But when a player shoots, the probability is that they are not going to score. It is the one aspect of soccer where failure is much more likely than success. Yet we want our players to keep trying to score, because if they don't we will probably lose the game.

A lot of mental strength is needed to take a shot in soccer. As coaches, one of our jobs is to make sure all of our players possess an abundance of this characteristic. Once we have the mental side of our players sorted, then we can focus on technique, on reading the game, on developing the weaker foot, on learning to shift the ball to create space for a shot. At the time of writing Erling Haaland has scored forty two goals for Manchester City. Included here is the remarkable feat of netting five goals in just thirty minutes against FC Leipzig (he was then taken off, before more damage could be inflicted) and he has netted numerous hat tricks. We are a fraction over two thirds of the season in, and he plays mostly in what is probably the most competitive league in the world, the English Premier League, and the cup competition with the best teams, the Champions League. In fact, in the earlier rounds of the lower level competitions such as the FA Cup, he often starts on the bench. And is still on target for fifty in a season. Yet for all this he has received a lot of criticism in the press, as well as praise. He does not suit Manchester City's style, he should be scoring more. He has gone three games without scoring. He does not have enough touches through the game. Yet he has scored thirty-seven goals. What do the critics expect? (He also seems like a levelheaded, sensible and sporting man. Can he do nothing wrong?)

Players who take shots really do earn the inexplicable ire of others. As coaches, we need to ensure that does not apply in our teams. Not from parents on the side, who bemoan a shot and demand that the pass be played to their son or daughter, who after all would be bound to score…not from team mates whose youthful immaturity means their natural disappointment at a missed chance is hard to keep inside. And certainly not from us, as coaches, even when we see a beautiful move lost thanks to one pass too few, and one shot too early.

We have a chapter on mental strength coming up shortly. But confidence is the life blood of every skill and technique in soccer, none more so that shooting. We must do everything to promote it, and nothing to dent it. With that cautionary story made, let us look at ways in which we can help our players become even better when they decide it is time to go for goal.

Quite a few of our other drills include a shooting element, so we have decided to include here two drills which encourage rapid shooting on sight, there to encourage our players to 'have a pop' when the opportunity arises. The first drill, though, challenges the convention that drills must be active, dynamic and involve lots of activity for all. This is, we believe, one occasion when a drill can be individual and involve a bit of waiting around and watching. We can get away with it here because the outcomes of the activity can be so spectacular!

Drill: The Scissor Kick Shot

Use With: All ages.

Objectives: Perfect the technique of the scissor kick.

Equipment: Balls.

64

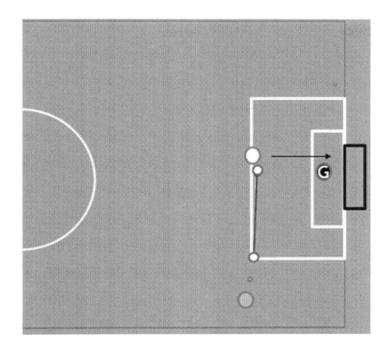

Operation of Drill: A feeder is needed, that is probably best undertaken by the coach as accuracy is needed. A goalkeeper also adds to the fun of the exercise, but this player must stay on their line to reduce any risk of injury to themselves or the kicker. The feeder gently lobs the ball into the penalty area with an underarm throw. The striker uses correct technique (see below) to strike the ball with a scissor kick.

65

Key Skills:

Technique is all.

- Face the ball chest on;
- As the ball comes in move to strike the ball at around knee height;
- Arms out for balance, legs slightly apart to provide a solid base;
- As the ball comes in, twist the hips so the arm pointing towards goal now points towards the ball;
- Judge the time to strike the ball:
- Rotate the arms and hips back towards the goal, creating a corkscrew motion;
- Keeping the arms out for balance, the outside foot swings at knee height to strike the ball with instep or laces.

Development:

- Try the overhead kick.

Drill: Shooting from Distance

This is a fairly complicated drill to set up and learn, but once in operation is extremely fluid and involves lots of players.

Use With: Older ages.

Objectives: Create space to shoot from distance.

Equipment: Balls.

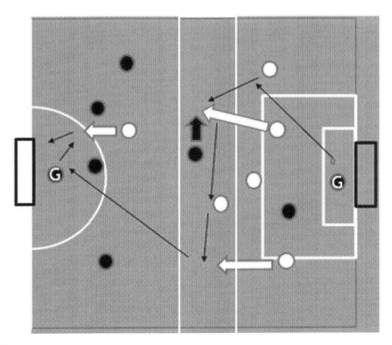

Operation of Drill:

- Two teams of seven. Each team has a goalkeeper, four defenders, a midfielder and a striker. The drill will work with six or eight a side. Add an extra striker with the larger numbers, or take a defender away if using smaller sides.

- Use half a pitch with a goal at each end. In the centre have a fairly narrow, say 10 metres deep, channel stretching across the width of the playing area.

- One player from each side is based in the midfield channel, and one striker per side is located in the opponents' defensive area. The other players begin in their own defensive zone.

- Play begins with the goal keeper.

- Once the goalie plays the ball to a team mate in their defensive zone, up to two further players from the side in possession can move into the midfield zone, creating an overload here or up to 3 v 1. This movement must be fluid and not pre-planned. Players work out who is best placed to move forward.

- The ball is eventually worked into the midfield zone. It does not matter how long this takes, or whether attackers move in and out of the zone, provided the allocated midfielder always remains there, and there are no more than three midfielders from the attacking side in the zone.

- Once in the midfield zone, the attack use their numerical advantage to work the ball into space.
- Once achieved they shoot from distance, from within the midfield zone.
- Their striker is alert for rebounds.
- If the ball is lost in the midfield zone, the midfielder who wins the ball can either shoot or play the ball back.
- If possession changes, during this transition the now defense must retreat back to their 4-1-1 formation, and the team who have won the ball can flood the midfield if they wish, within the rules of the drill.
- After a shot play continues with the defense becoming the attack and the goalkeeper once more beginning the move.

Key Skills:

- Communication.
- Tactical awareness to make best use of the midfield overload.
- Shooting technique.

- Being alert to the development of play (tactical awareness).

Development:

- Increase the numbers in the midfield zone to reduce space.

Drill: Rapid Fire

This is a fast moving drill which replicates the pressure of shooting in a match situation.

Use With: All ages.

Objectives: Move the ball quickly to create shooting opportunities.

Equipment: Balls.

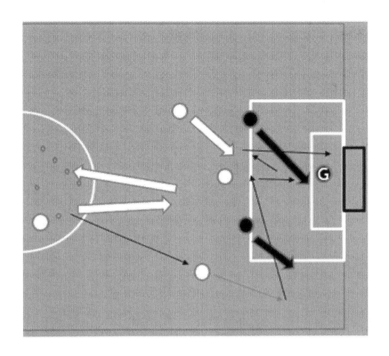

Operation of Drill: This is a rondo style drill with 4 v 2 plus a goalkeeper. The attackers have three minutes to score as many goals as they can. One point for getting off a shot, three points for shooting on target and five points for scoring a goal.

Use half a pitch. The two defenders begin in their penalty area. The attackers can begin anywhere. The balls are placed in the halfway line semi-circle. A player fetches a ball and passes or dribbles at speed. Team mates move to stretch the defense and create space for a shot.

71

The attacking team shoots when it thinks it is in the best position to score.

After a shot, an attacker returns to the semi-circle to start another attack with a different ball. The coach should be active in this drill, pointing out space and movement. So it is a drill which works best if an assistant can work with the rest of the group on a different activity, allowing the coach to concentrate on the players' movements and skills.

Key Skills:

- Communication.
- Movement to create space.
- Moving the ball quickly to replicate transition in a match situation.
- Shooting technique.

Development:

- Add an extra defender.

Drill: Control and Shoot

A more challenging drill here, which requires players to control passes and crosses from a variety of angles and received at different heights. The first touch is very important. It should bring the ball down and allow for a rapid shot, either with the next movement or after a maximum of one more touch. Where 'feeders' struggle to chip or lift the ball with control, allow them to lob the ball in under arm to ensure more accuracy. However, some passes should be along the ground played with the instep.

Use With: Any age. Younger players in our age group may find the drill too tricky.

Objectives: Control a pass or cross and unleash a shot in as few touches as possible.

Equipment: Balls, goal.

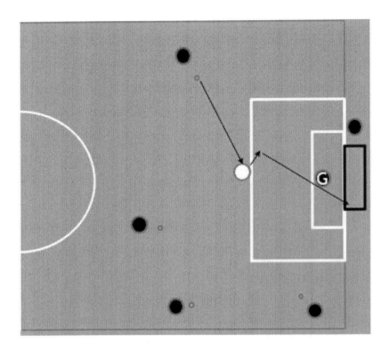

Operation of Drill: Place four feeders ten to twenty metres from the striker. Striker is positioned on the edge of the box. Fifth feeder returns balls so that the action is non-stop. Feeders choose height at which to deliver the ball, but the coach ensures there is variety suitable to the age and ability of the player. Striker controls the ball, and shoots with as few additional touches as possible. After an attempt from each feeder swap positions. Keep rotating until all have had a go in each position. Repeat.

Key Skills:

- Feeders pass accurately, and if able to control the skill, provide a variety of chips, driven passes and passes along the ground.
- Striker moves feet to get into position to control the ball:
  o Chest control;
  o Spread arms to make as broad a chest area as possible,
  o Slightly point chest down at point of contact to ensure the ball does not move away from the player,
  o The ball is likely to bounce. Either strike with laces on the volley or half volley or take a second touch to bring the ball under complete control.
    ▪ Ensure arms for balance,
    ▪ Plant the non-kicking foot around six inches to the side of the striking point,
    ▪ Head over the ball,
    ▪ Knee of striking leg slightly bent,
    ▪ Strike through the ball, using the laces (instep for lob), and extend the kicking foot smoothly,

- There is no need to hit the ball too hard. Get the technique right and the power will come.
  o Strike with the laces, using good shooting technique as described elsewhere or
  o Place the shot using the instep.

Development:

- Add a defender to pressure the striker.

A question coaches are often asked is whether to practice penalties or not. On the one hand, they do not involve a huge amount of activity from the whole group. But on the other, they are fun, everybody loves a shootout. So, yes, practising this skill is fine. A good way to integrate it is to use a shootout after the final whistle of the end of session game. Even if there is a winner to this, the final score can count after the shootout. There is no hard and fast method to taking a good penalty. Useful techniques include clearing the mind to focus only on the ball. Visualise where the shot will go. Strike with the instep, using good technique. If using the laces, make sure the head stays over the ball. Decide beforehand where the shot will go and stick to this. Of course, we are seeing a change to the penalty technique where players often now pause during the run up and try to see where the goalkeeper is going. There is nothing wrong with allowing players to try out their own methods, including the Panenka. If the goalie guesses they will end up looking a bit daft, and will probably never try one again. For once, that might be a good thing!

Tactical Awareness

The extent to which we use tactics with children is one of those debates which evoke strong emotions among many coaches. At one extreme are those who argue that without tactics players are gaining only a small insight to the intricacies of soccer. On the other are the advocates who believe that young players must focus on enjoyment, the acquisition of skills and the development of technique.

We do not sit on either edge of the argument. Tactics are becoming something children can understand as they enter the age range covered by this book. By under twelve level, keen players will watch the adult game and will be picking up on tactics used by coaches, so it is perfectly legitimate to introduce them to the concept that a match might be won or lost by the strategies employed by players and coaches. After all, even the concept that one player is a striker, whilst another has a more defensive role is an example of tactics employed at the simplest level. At the same time, we do not advocate lengthy team talks with a tactics board and complex instructions regarding what a player can do or not do during the game. Definitely, even at under eight level, make sure that players know their job, but do not make that job too restrictive.

Drill: Making a Run to Create Space

A key aim in soccer is to create an imbalance of players. Indeed, rondo drills are in part a recognition of the importance of exploiting this situation when it occurs. This simple drill illustrates the value of making runs. It is fast paced and requires plenty of repetition so that it becomes second nature for players to make such runs.

Use With: All ages, although the drill works better with older players.

Objectives: Make a run to create space for a team mate.

Equipment: Balls.

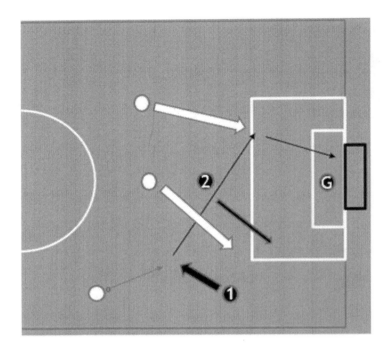

Operation of Drill: Three attackers, two defenders and a goalkeeper. The defenders must carry out their jobs. Defender 1 tries to win the ball off the player in possession, defender 2 must track the run of the centre forward. The central attacker makes a run which opens up space for a team mate to have an opportunity to shoot on goal.

Key Skills:

- Timing the run so it is not too early or late.
- Shooter times run to move into space vacated.

80

- Dribbler releases the ball when the space is created and the defender is on the move, covering the run. Too late and they may be tackled, too early and the central defender can recover and stop the shot.
- Communication between attackers important to help with the timing outlined above.

Development:

- Play this as a 3 v 3 game, with defenders not conditioned as above. If the run is not tracked, then the pass can be made to the runner as they will be in space.

Drill: The Inverted Full Back

With our age of players matches are usually small-sided affairs. These provide more opportunity for time on the ball and the perfection of skills and technique. That is a good thing. However, by under twelve level teams are often made up of nine players, which certainly brings the concept of an inverted full back into play, and even at under eleven, a seven a side game may see a team line up with ostensibly three defenders. In fact, this formation requires the tactical awareness of the defence to move into midfield when in possession, something central to the principle of the inverted full back.

It is a role simple to explain but challenging to perform. However, a good young player with growing tactical awareness will be able to undertake the position. When in position one of the full backs advances into midfield and adopts a deepish (or even advanced) central midfield role. This gives an overload to the team in possession in this crucial part of the field, and either creates times for an effective pass or dribble or draws a defender into the midfield region creating space for more attacking players.

Using a player in this role is very much the tactic of the moment. In the English Premier League, Arsenal have caused a huge shock by challenging the traditional hegemony of Manchester City and a curiously out of form Liverpool, and at the time of writing lead the league by eight points. An absolutely key factor in this has been the form of their left back, Oleksandr Zinchenko, who operates as an inverted full back. This means that, in possession, the player not only supports the midfield but instead of doing so from a traditionally wide position, he cuts inside to make an additional threat in central midfield. This brings a number of benefits tactically to a team. There is a spare player in central midfield who can not only add to the attack, but be an extra block should possession be lost and transition occur. It means the wide players can remain wide, where they are more effective than a full back in the position. This also creates width and hence space for central players. Creative central midfielders can also relinquish the more defensive aspects of their game and do what they do best – producing opportunities for their strikers.

Of course there is a risk. A quick transition can leave space at the back, albeit in a wide rather than central position. But the benefits of using this tactic clearly outweigh the risks. However, a full back working in inverted role must be able to read the game well and be competent on the ball.

Use With: Older age groups within the 8-12 range.

Objectives: Overload midfield by using the inverted full back

Equipment: Normal pitch

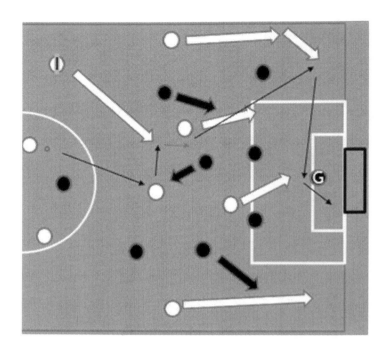

(Note: diagram shows attack half only. Inverted full back marked with 'I')

Operation of Drill: This is a conditioned nine a side match practice (the drill can be adapted to incorporate seven a side games) which sees various players acting as the inverted full backs. Thus, they learn about the role whilst their coach can see which players perform the function best. For the conditioned element of the game, begin each break down with an unpressured restart from the defensive third and allow a pass

84

into midfield unopposed, so the full back can move into their inverted position.

Key Skills:

- Awareness of the game, and especially when to move forward and inside, and when to drop back.
- Wide players stay wide to create space.

Development:

- Develop into a normal game, without condition.

Drill: Effective Transition

Many goal scoring opportunities come from transition events. This is where a team gains possession from their opponents. Often, because the opponents have been on the offensive they are vulnerable to a counter attack if it is carried out at pace because their own defense is out of position.

Use With: All ages, although probably this drill works best with under tens and upwards.

Objectives: Win possession and break at speed to create a threatening counter attack.

Equipment: Two thirds of a pitch, three small goals, normal goal, ball, cones.

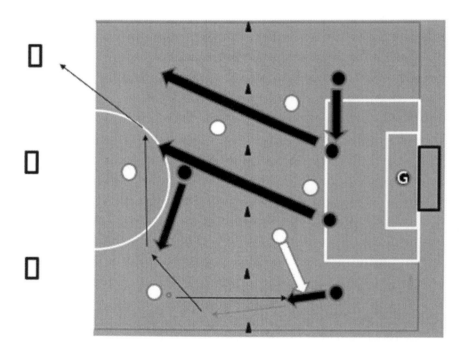

(Note: for this drill, defence becomes attack and vice versa. The colour used in the arrows and circles represent the initial role of the two sides.)

Operation of Drill: This is a conditioned six a side match practice. The offensive side have six outfield players and the defence five outfield players and a goal keeper. The playing area is divided into two. There are several variations of rules compared to a normal game, best explained with bullet points.

1. The defensive side have three small goals to attack if and when they win possession in their own defensive half. This is the transition element of the drill.

2. The offensive side attack a normal goal.

3. Only one player from the defense is permitted in their opponents' half UNTIL the ball is either passed or dribbled by the defense into this half. At that point, the defense can attack.

4. The game is played for five minutes, then the sides swap roles.

5. The defence cannot be awarded a corner, free kick or penalty, otherwise normal rules apply.

6. Each time an attack breaks down, the ball is returned to the offensive team to begin their attack from one of their goals.

After each five minute session, the coach briefly discusses what worked well and encourages both sides to give their own feedback. This way, the players begin to learn effective transition techniques. For example, the role of wide defenders breaking to support the attack can be very important, whilst the opposite full back coming inside and remaining as a defender can also help to reduce threats if possession is lost quickly after the transition.

Key Skills:

- Communication with teammates.
- Attacking in numbers when transition occurs, whilst retaining an awareness that possession can be lost again, exposing the team to danger.
- Counter attacking at speed to reduce the opportunity for opponents to re-organise.

Development:

- Move onto a normal match situation but condition the game to encourage fast counter attacks on transition.

Drill: Creating the Overlap

Repetition is the key with this drill. The full back should feel comfortable breaking forward, understanding that they may or may not get the pass. Indeed, each player has a role which may result in them receiving the ball, or not. However, unless they understand that their job is important irrespective of whether they do eventually receive the ball, the tactic will not become ingrained. Players should learn that their running creates space and opportunities for their teammates and causing the defense problems. Many variations of the drill can be used. Coaches can design their own adaptations to the basic set up below.

Use With: All ages.

Objectives: Work as a three to create an overlap for the full back. If the overlap is not used with a pass, then the movement itself causes the defense to become stretched and out of position. Three attackers face two defenders and a keeper. The aim is to make an overlapping run and from this create a goal scoring opportunity.

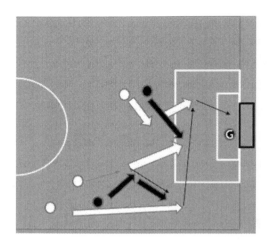

Example One, central striker makes a far post run

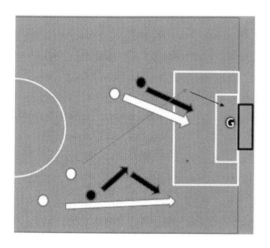

Example Two, central striker makes a near post run, dribbler
moves into space to shoot

The dribbler cuts inside taking their defender with them. The full back breaks into the space left by the full back. If the defense picks up this run, space is created elsewhere. The central striker makes a run. Run one is towards the far past. Now either the final defender must track the run, leaving space elsewhere, or covers the space and leaves this player unmarked. Run two would be to the near post, which allows the dribbler to drive towards the far post and either release a shot themselves, or, if they have already laid the ball off to the full back, then be unmarked in this position. In either case, the striker bends their run, cutting briefly in one direction before accelerating in the opposite direction.

If the full back is not covered, they simply drive at the goal themselves.

This drill is about good decision making. The defense should really cover the biggest threats, which means heading towards the ball and the nearest player. Therefore, most space should come at the far post. To keep the drill realistic to the match situation, it should be carried out at speed. For the attacking side, the best decisions are about utilising the space the overlap creates. There will always be a player unmarked and in space. Players look to use this player rather than using dribbling skills to beat the defender.

Equipment: Half pitch, ball.

Operation of Drill: The points here are broadly covered above but listed as bullet points to make them clearer and easier to explain to the young players.

- Dribbler attacks at speed, driving infield.
- Full back sprints down the wing, passing the dribbler.
- Central striker decides on their run, and makes it in line with the description above.
- Dribbler decides on the best option:
  - Pass to the overlapping full back, because they are unmarked,
  - Pass to the central striker because they are unmarked,
  - Continue the run themselves, ending in a shot, because the defence has split to cover the runners.
- Defense attempts to react to the movement and make the attempt at goal as difficult as possible.
- Have three attempts and then change roles.
- Keep rotating until all have tried in each position.

Key Skills:

- Dribbling at speed.
- Finding Space
- Decision making – the focus here is on the attack, but the coach should also advise and comment on the defense's decision making.
- Shooting.

Development:

- If the offensive side are finding it difficult to get in a shot, add an additional striker.
- Develop the drill to a full game, stopping to point out effective use of the overlapping run, and also where the opportunity arose but was missed.

It is time to move away from specifically soccer related drills for a short while. When working with relatively young children, it helps the coach if they have some understanding of the physical and mental well-being of their players.

Reward 2:

As a reward for reading this chapter on tactical awareness, we wanted to give you a bonus that you will enjoy. It's a book on Soccer Intelligence that looks at different skills and strategies to improve a player's awareness on the field. Just scan the QR code below to get your book.

Physical Fitness

Being physically fit is not only essential for a player to keep running for the duration of the game, but it helps with mental fitness as well. Mistakes creep in when players are physically tired. That is because concentration slips and errors follow. Only 7% of goals on average are scored in the first ten minutes of a game, the lowest of any ten-minute spell, whilst typically almost a third of goals (29%) are scored in the final twenty. So, physical fitness is a key weapon in a soccer player's armoury.

Except, lack of physical fitness is rarely an issue for pre-adolescent children. Watch youngsters. They are constantly on the move; they run everywhere. Admittedly, the growth of online games is challenging this truth, but it is still unusual that an under twelve or younger needs to spend any time on physical conditioning. If they do, the problem is likely to be as much psychological as physical, which is an area in which most amateur coaches are unqualified to work. However, whilst the good news is that most coaches working with our age range will not have to plan lengthy fitness drills, it does not mean that fitness exercises should play no part in a coach's training programme. After all, we are helping our players to get into good habits for life. Whilst they might not need too much fitness work at the age of eight or ten, we can help train them into keeping healthy so that when they are older, and do need such conditioning, it is easier to apply it.

Therefore we have some drills which do help with physical fitness, because they are extremely active, but which also focus as much, if not more, on soccer skills. Thus our players get the best of both worlds. The focus on these drills is fun. After all, when our players are older, and face the unpleasant thought of a couple of hours in the gym, we want them to have as positive a mindset towards this as they can!

Drill: Soccer Circuits

Circuit training with a difference. Set up the drills in advance, as this can be a little time consuming. By repeating the same drills regularly, and recording players times to complete a circuit, they can measure their own progress and see if they can complete the drills ever more quickly. This will mean that not only is their fitness improving, but their skill level too.

Use With: All players.

Objectives: Hone skills whilst developing fitness.

Equipment: As required.

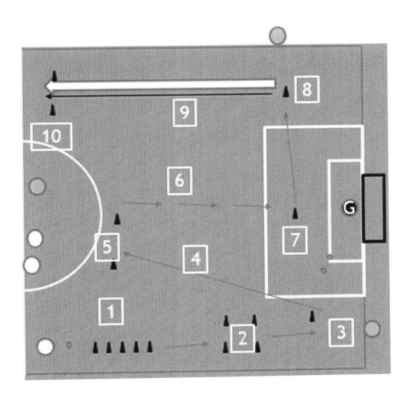

Operation of Drill: Start players off once the previous participant has completed enough of the course that they will not be overtaken.

This will naturally lead to a rest between rotations. Complete three to five rotations of the drill per session.

The example above contains ten drills, for three rotations. A few helpers are needed. The drills are:

1. Dribble through cones, then dribble on to…
2. Five juggles, then dribble on to…
3. Five wall passes with a coach (in this example of a circuit, once a player has completed this drill it would be a good time to set the next player off. After a while, all participants are either on the circuit, or recovering from their exertions…) Then dribble on to…
4. Running with the ball
5. Four Cruyff turns, then dribble on to…
6. Skill run – dribble with the ball performing three 'skills' en route – eg step over, 360 turn, feint, then dribble on to…
7. Penalties (have spare balls here in case of a penalty that misses the target), continue until player scores, then dribble on to…
8. Controlling throw ins, player receives throw in to chest, they control and return, then knee height, then to feet.

Fourth throw into weaker foot, which is controlled and player turns…

9. Long pass through gate, If missed, player collects ball and tries again from half the distance…

10. Sprint through the gate without ball. Time recorded as player passes through the gate.

Key Skills: As per the drills

Development: Drills can be adapted to work on areas identified by the coach as needing attention, although this might preclude the idea of players keeping a running record of their times.

Drill: Non-Stop Dribbling

This is a slight misnomer, as mostly there will be breaks in activity although it is possible that a player may have to dribble continuously for the duration of the drill.

Use With: All players.

Objectives: Improve close control dribbling skills whilst improving leg strength and fitness.

Equipment: Balls, one per player.

Operation of Drill: Depending on numbers, create a grid which will be tight but not impossible to work within. In the example here, one 20 m x 15m will suffice. Working with thirteen players, choose four to begin as 'tunnels'. (Try to keep a similar 1 to 3 ratio however many players are doing the drill). These 'tunnels' stand still with their legs apart. One player is earmarked as 'defender'. We will come to him or her shortly. The other players must dribble moving continuously. The dribblers must dribble the ball through the legs of a 'tunnel'. Dribblers shout the number of the tunnels they have passed through. One a dribbler reaches five she swaps with the last 'tunnel' through which she has passed.

Meanwhile, the defender is attempting to tackle players and kick their ball out of the grid. If for any reason the ball goes out of the grid, that player begins again on '0'. Each successful tackle is shouted by the defender, and when they reach ten they can swap with any 'tunnel' of their choosing.

This exercise does not lend itself to a diagram but is hopefully clear. It is a great deal of fun, and a player could be expecting a welcome rest with a short period as a tunnel when they are immediately replaced by the latest dribbler to pass through them!

Key Skills:

- Close dribbling skills.

Development:

- Add a second defender.

Drill: Soccer Skill Relays

Everybody loves a relay race, and we can combine the fun of the competition with some work on fitness whilst practising a skill at the same time. The example here is a wall pass relay, but the drill works with dribbling relays, running with the ball relays where the player at the back sprints to the front, receives a pass and then passes onto the player who supersedes them at the front. In fact, coaches will come up with all sorts of variations on the theme.

Use With: All ages.

Objectives: First time pass with accuracy in a pressure and fitness situation.

Equipment: Balls, cones.

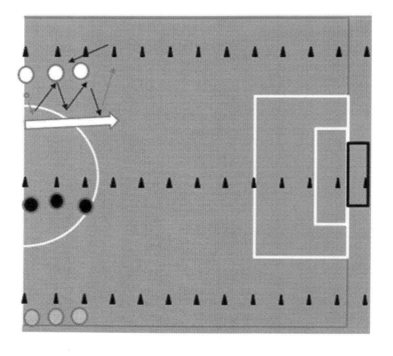

Diagram shows movement of white team. Black and grey teams are doing the same, racing to see who finishes first

Operation of Drill: Any number of players per team. Cones across the pitch. Players by the first cones in their line. The player by the first cone begins the drill. He dribbles away from the cones for five metres, then conducts a series of first-time wall passes (allow more touches as appropriate) with teammates, progressing along the line of players. When he reaches the end of the line, he dribbles to the next cone, then passes back to the player now at the back of the line. The drill is repeated until the first team reaches the end of the line of cones and wins.

Key Skills:

- Body position to receive pass ready to lay off first time.
- Pass firmly with instep, making sure the ball stays on the ground.
- Head over ball when passing.
- Players by cone pass slightly in front of team mate so they do not have to break stride.

Development:

- Reduce touches or increase distance of passes.

Drill: Another Soccer Skill Relay – Dribble and Pass

Use With: Any age.

Objectives: Dribble to a cone, pass back. First team to pass through the end gate wins.

Equipment: Half pitch, cones, balls.

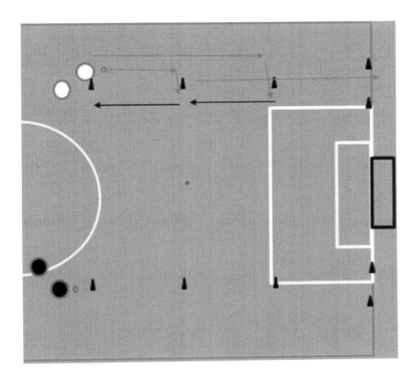

Operation of Drill: Set cones around 20 metres apart along the length of half a pitch. Divide the teams into twos, threes or fours. The smaller the teams the more physical exercise is undertaken. Player one dribbles to the first cone. Turns, and passes back to the team mate. They dribble onto the next cone, passing the first player, and pass back. Keep going until a player dribbles through the gate. Depending on the number of players, the lengths of the dribbles will vary.

Key Skills:

- Dribbling and running with the ball.
- Stopping the ball and turning quickly. Good players will use a trick such as the Cruyff turn to change direction.
- Accurate passing with the instep.
- First touch.

Development:

- Add cones to dribble between or offset cones to change the angle of passing and dribbling.

In the next chapter we will take a look at developing mental strength in our players, whilst touching on some of the conditions from which some of our players may suffer, and how these may impact on their performance and behaviour during training and matches.

Mental Exercises and Emotional Development

Remember that day at the Hofmeister's barbeque? Sun warm on our heads, one Bud (other chilled lagers are available) too many, the sweet taste of the marinade on the slightly charred chicken? Probably not. But if you do, or something similar, you'll have marked it as the point you agreed to run the under tens, and your weekends changed. Forever. For the better, of course. Your weekday nights as well. Because if you are not actually running a session, or coaching a match, then you are planning, or reviewing.

What we mostly do not expect when we sign the dotted line and promise our lives to the icon that is soccer is that we will have to become experts not only in playing the sport, not just in designing ways of passing on that expertise - methods which keep our players interested and happy, but also become semi-practitioners in the field of child emotional development. Does it help if, such is the case with many coaches of youth soccer teams, we have children of our own? Well, a bit. But not that much. Certainly, it means we might be a bit more familiar with the latest lingo or even get that One Direction is not an option on Google Maps, or that Harry Styles isn't actually a clothes shop on the High Street. But conversely, we all sit in the hope that our Joanna or Johnnie is a normal, popular kid; we all have those moments in our darkest times when we fear that they are not, and what we will learn very quickly is that there is no such thing as a 'normal' kid. Each is unique, each has their own triggers and traumas and talents.

In taking a brief look at this field of emotional development in eight to twelve year olds we should hold that essential truth in the forefront of all we do. Every child is different, and whilst it is true that some general behaviours can be popular, and others generally unwelcome, we should hold on to the fact that if eighty per cent of the group are loving a particular approach, the remaining twenty per cent who are standing there, quiet and reflective, may be not having a good time at all. Take banter as an example. Many kids love a bit of banter, enjoy the attention of being subject to it and so forth. For some, though, the horror of being singled out ruins an evening. The fear that it might happen can haunt them for days before. What we also may, or may not, know is that a particular child has a condition which makes them neuro-divergent, meaning they think, perceive and rationalise events and situations differently to most of their peers. What is a joke to one child can be a devastating put down to another.

It's tough. Tough for us as coaches, and even more challenging for our players. If only we could focus purely on soccer things would be easier, but we know that children grow holistically. Their soccer will probably be one of the most significant and, hopefully, enjoyable parts of their week. We can offer so much to their growth as young people if we have an understanding of how they are perceiving their experiences.

We will take a look at the following areas. We will consider how children's brains develop in this pre and early pubescent stage of their lives. We will take a look at the social and emotional changes they will be facing, including that dreaded moment when a mood swing hits. Included here will be some of the social changes our players may be facing as they grow physically and emotionally. We will briefly analyse the development of resilience and the growth of confidence which soccer can do so much to promote. We will compare some of the gender differences which exist when coaching boys and girls, and touch briefly on two of the disorders from which our players could suffer – autism (ASD) and ADHD. Finally, we will consider some of the risky behaviours we may encounter as coaches. Where appropriate, we'll suggest some exercises a coach can use to help children with their emotional development.

Brain Development in Eight to Twelve Year Olds

Even if we are coaching children as young as under eights, our players' brains are pretty much completely developed. They are at about 95% of a fully formed adult brain. In fact, most of the changes now will be about getting rid of the bits of the brain that prove to be unnecessary (evolution having rendered them redundant), while the connections which lead to cognitive decisions are strengthened. This process begins at the rear of the brain. Something which is a bit of an evolutionary error. Because the final bit of the brain to undergo its makeover is the front, specifically the pre-frontal cortex. That is the part of our grey matter which adults use to make decisions. To decide whether they can pull out before the car on the left arrives, to choose to smile in the face of the aggressive drunk who has just bumped into their arm in the pub. Children still make decisions, but tend to rely on the amygdala, which is a section mostly concerned with emotions, aggression and instinct.

Which explains why children lash out under pressure, become surprisingly emotional about what seem to be minor matters. So when we, as an adult coach, say quite reasonably that our centre forward should have passed rather tried a thirty yard shot (…not forgetting that we encourage shooting!) we might be surprised when our ten year old striker tears up, and is moody for the remainder of the session. That is his emotional response to the criticism. He can't help it. It's a fault of evolution, and no matter how we try we are not going to change thirty thousand years of human development in a forty minute training session on a Wednesday night.

However, there are some things we can do to help.

Tips and Suggestions One to Four:

- Be positive all of the time, even when things are not going well. Remember children read expressions and body language as well as words, albeit with far from certain accuracy. Even if we cannot always deduce a child's reaction, we can reduce the opportunity for a negative emotional response to a situation.
- During each session hold a 'positive feedback' moment. Here we go around our players, and ask them to say something positive about a particular players' performance. It must be positive, with no 'but' clause involved. We might find that our players begin to run out of original things to say, and if we think that is happening after four or five responses then we can keep an eye out for someone who is ready to say something (don't ask for

volunteers, a 'no response' somewhat spoils the moment). You can usually tell who is waiting to speak from their own focus and body language, which will hyper alert, even tense. Then, if not everybody has contributed choose another child to praise and continue with comments about them.

- One of the challenges young people face with brain development and decision making is that they find risk extremely hard to assess. Many clubs have 'end of season' outings or tours. Include 'controlled risk' activities such as abseiling, climbing, caving or canoeing rather than another trip to the Pizza palace. This gives children a chance to learn about risk in a safe environment. Remember that saying with which we started – 'I do and I understand'; do the risk and you understand it.

- Keep coaching soccer. Lots of research indicates that sport is an excellent outlet for children to expend their emotions positively and creatively.

Social and Emotional Changes

At this age children will begin to consider their own identity, and where it fits within their world. This will often take the form of them trying out new fashions (although that can be bit more of a teenage fad) or making new friends. They will also be keen to take responsibility, and beware, children of this age take their responsibilities extremely seriously. Woe betide a coach who drops litter, or forgets to turn the lights off in the club house. We also see a shift away from a dependence on adults for social guidance, and peer pressure plays a much bigger role in our players' lives. While they will still very much be influenced by what we say, at the upper end of our age range this is just beginning to waver, and if we take a team through for a three or four years, we will find that some of our decisions begin to be questioned. Probably not studiously ignored, but not accepted with quite the willingness of previously. Once we understand that most probably a mood swing is down to emotional growth and not spoiled brat syndrome (although, sometimes, it is…) we can cope better and be less concerned by the change in temperament.

Again, first and foremost we must be aware of these emotional developments, but there are mental health exercises and practices we can use which will assist our players' progress.

Tips and Suggestions Five to Eight:

- Give players responsibilities. Get them to lead small groups during drills or have jobs such as arriving early to set up drills, clearing up at the end. If parents agree, phoning round to check if anybody is not going to be able to attend a session is a valuable responsibility, as is pumping balls and so forth.

- Rotate captaincy. There is not a really good reason why the same child needs to wear the armband each week. So share it about, give every child a chance to be captain for a game or two.

- Play 'What would you do?'. This can be soccer related, but then move onto wider decision making, helping players to make choices. We can then talk about these choices (briefly). Often, we will find this sort of activity encourages a player to wait behind at the end of the session and share a concern or a story.
  - The game is simple and can be designed with a few minutes preparation.
  - Write down a few dilemmas. Read one out, ask for responses.

- For example, you are the penalty taker, but your friend needs cheering up. Do you let them take the penalty?
- A player forgets their boots and is worried they will be in trouble. What do you do?
- Pass or dribble, which is best?
- A player is injured but is desperate to play on. What do you advise?

- Organise groups for drills, rather than allow players to pick their own groups. This ensures better mixture of players. Or, if this is how a session normally works, allow players to pick their own groups, and try out friendships for themselves. Although, beware of a child being left out. Especially if numbers do not quite work.

Resilience and Confidence

Resilience is the ability we develop to cope with adversity and setbacks and come back from disappointments. We can contribute a lot to children's acquisition of this essential life skill, and in fact are doing so just by giving them the chance to be a part of a team. Through this they will develop social skills and learn to develop new friendships and meet new people. They will experience winning and losing and are taking part in a sport where even the best teams and strongest players make errors.

Each of these provide opportunities for developing resilience. All that is needed is the right philosophy and mindset from the players. Something which comes down to the coach.

Tips and Suggestions Eight to Fourteen:

- Encourage players to make decisions.
- Do not criticise when a player makes a decision, even when it goes wrong. Instead, praise them for making a choice.
- Do not allow an atmosphere of blame to develop. If a bad pass occurs, acknowledge the attempt rather than criticise the delivery.
- Prioritise praise for decision making during post-match feedback sessions, even if the decision went wrong. Ask what a player has learned, or how them might achieve their goal more successfully next time.
- Encourage players to watch professionals. Rarely now do we see frustrated arm waving from players when a teammate makes a bad decision or delivers a weak pass.

Instead, we see players congratulating the intent if not the result. This approach delivers a powerful message for our young players.

- Do not allow parents and spectators to create a negative atmosphere which deters players from trying skills or making creative decisions. Achieving this can be difficult, and a coach may need support from the club hierarchy with particularly challenging parents.

- End sessions with a 'What have we learned?' plenary. Go round the group, asking for one aspect of their play they think will have improved during the session. When first introduced players may find it hard to come up with ideas. This will be a reflection of their own lack of confidence, but they will soon learn to focus on positives and opportunities. That is because they know they will be asked about them at the end.

Reasonably enough, the positive growth of girls' football is going to leave a lot of coaches wondering about the differences of teaching the genders. Increasingly at our age range teams are becoming mixed, although the vast majority still remain single sex. We should not lose sight of the fact that girls begin puberty earlier than boys, and it is far from unusual to have girls of nine, or even younger, beginning their menstruation cycles, with all the considerations such development brings. Sympathy, understanding and trust are the jobs of the coach here. Don't allow a policy, for example, when non-attendance at a training session means a player is dropped for the following game. It might well not be the player's fault. To be fair, most coaches will have designated dropping players for non-attendance and such like to the bin where the old leather balls and crossbars made of tape are kept.

Consider the colour of the team kit – darker is better where possible - and allow wearing of tracksuit bottoms in any conditions.

Neurodiversity

This is the term which covers the range of brain function and behaviours we can expect to see amongst the population. It is an important term, because it shows that there is a continuum upon which people sit, proving any concept of 'normality' to be completely inappropriate and, often, dangerous. Certainly, there are a range of behaviours which are more common among the general population, but to look for any uniformity among these is to search for a pot of gold at the end of the rainbow. Not only will the gold fail to be there, but a lot of time will be wasted forlornly searching for the tip of the brightly coloured but non-existent band.

Within our group we will therefore see a range of behaviours and perceptions from our players. We will have children who appear very confident, others who are withdrawn, some who love attention and others who might shy away from it. Some of our players will be deeply sensitive towards their peers' reactions to anything they do, or say, or wear, or attempt. Others will have little regard for such considerations. And so on.

Speak to a good teacher and they will explain that whilst a lesson might be pitched towards a class, or the majority of it, the expectations of what constitute success or otherwise for that lesson varies from student to student. It is the same for our planning. We might organise some special sessions for a player to work on a particular skill where they are lacking, while the rest do something else. We more commonly might deliver goalkeeper only drills, or drills for the defense or attack. It will depend a lot on our resources in terms of facilities, equipment and staff. But whether we have one drill going for everybody, or multiple activities, we must keep in our heads that each of our players will react differently to them. What constitutes a success for one player might not be quite such a stringent bar for another.

With that in mind, it is easier to be positive, and positivity is the key to success when working with neurodiverse players. We also accept

119

that sometimes behaviour might be challenging, or worrying and we may be concerned that some children are not enjoying sessions. It is hard to say. If they keep turning up, the chances are that they are having fun. Just, not everybody shows this in the same way.

People study for years, acquire Masters' Degrees, undergo lengthy training in order to help neurodiverse children. We are soccer coaches. We know a bit about the sport, want to give children a chance to play and work hard to give them a productive and enjoyable time. We are not psychologists or counsellors or mental health professionals. It would be dangerous if we thought we were. We'd advise (and these are the next four tips. **Numbers Fifteen to Eighteen.**)

- Talking to parents if we have concerns.
- No preconceived expectations.
- Keep encouraging.
- Keep smiling. We do as much good as we possibly can just with those four actions.

But the fact is that there might be times when we are very concerned about any child's behaviour. We become a significant adult in our player's lives, and that means there is a chance that a boy or girl may make a disclosure to us. In that situation our actions are clear. This is not a suggestion, or a tip, but an action all adults in a position of responsibility should follow, because the interests of the child overshadow all else.

These days a club will have a written policy on dealing with safeguarding issues. It might go under any of a number of headings: child protection, child safety, safeguarding, protecting children and so forth. We should know the procedures outlined in that policy, and we must follow them. Simple as that. Whatever the disclosure. There are broadly four types of abuse which will be covered by the policy. These are sexual, physical, emotional and neglect. Again, headings may be different. The final two are often harder to define, and harder to assess, but no less serious than the first two. If in doubt, pass it on. Hopefully, as a coach we will never find ourselves in this position, but we might. It is horrible, and stressful and upsetting.

It might appear as though this chapter has focussed on just a minority of our players. Some small groups. It hasn't. When it comes to mental health, and drills to encourage mental strength, every member of our team is a group. A very small one, made up of just themselves. We are all different. Just, it has taken a long time for us to recognise this truth.

Enough of this difficult and challenging aspect which might arise with our players and onto a topic much more related to what we want to deliver as soccer coaches. Teamwork.

Reward 3:

As a reward for completing this chapter, I'd like to offer you my free book on "Soccer Mental Toughness". It's a book on skills, strategies and exercises to use your mind to improve performances on the field. Just scan the QR code to get your book.

Developing Teamwork

A bit of variety does everybody some good, so we have some activities here which are not specifically soccer related, but which are great for developing teamwork. We would not advocate using these sorts of activities more than once every five or six weeks, after all the team have come for a soccer session, not a teamwork session. We'd also say it is worth explaining clearly why the group are trying the activity. The children will enjoy them, and usually they take around ten minutes to complete.

Activity One: Developing Communication

This requires some equipment most coaches will be able to get their hands on. Some building bricks are required, plus some tables or benches so the team members cannot see what their team mates are doing.

Use With: All ages. The older the children, the larger the number of bricks that can be used.

Objectives: Use effective communication to replicate a building.

Equipment: Ten to twelve building bricks, exactly replicated with a copy. One set of these doubles for each team. For younger players use six or seven building bricks.

Operation of Drill: Divide the group into teams of four. Each player has a role. Player one is the architect, player two is the carrier, player three the fetcher, and player four the builder.

- The architect sits at one end of the pitch, facing away from their builder, and creates a shape using his or her bricks.
- The carrier must look at the building, then run to the half way line to communicate to the fetcher an exact copy of what has been built. Note, this is likely to take several journeys.
- The carrier runs to the builder and tells them to how build an exact replica, including colour, angle and building size of their architect's creation.
- The builder gradually builds the architect's creation.
- When the builder thinks they have finished, the fetcher hands the creation to the carrier, who gives it to the

architect. The buildings are compared. If correct, the team are finished.

- If there are errors, the building is returned to the builder and the communications continue until the shape is right.

Key Skills:

- Accurate, clear and concise communication. Players learn quickly that simple, unambiguous instruction is needed.

Development:

- The game can be adapted to any sort of building, painting or drawing.

Communication is vital, and a cog in this engine which sometimes gets overlooked is the role played by listening. Active listening, in particular. This is where a person focusses intently on the information being given. A good way to check is to question a player after some instructions have been given. Nothing too pressurised, or that might put a person too much on the spot, but if players know they will be asked about what they have been told, they are likely to pay stronger attention.

The popular method of keeping kids quiet in the car can be used promote active listening. We don't mean give them a laptop and tell them to play games, but instead a soccer related version of the perennial 'I'm going on holiday and I am taking...' is a good one. Play occasionally just for three or four rounds, no need to find a winner, before giving team instructions. We will find our players' listening skills are honed.

Activity Two: During the match today I am going to...

Most coaches will know the game on which this is based, but for those who do not...

Use With: All ages.

Objectives: Encourage active listening through listening carefully to a repeated list.

Equipment: An active brain, especially from the coach (or maybe a list to refer to when needed)...

Operation of Drill: Coach begins by saying: 'During the game today I am going to... encourage everybody. The next player repeats what the

127

coach has said, and then adds another item of his or her own. And so on.

If a player cannot think of everything, the coach helps out, because the idea is not to find a winner, but to get brains in gear for active listening. Suggestions include:

- Score a goal.
- Make a save.
- Win a tackle.
- Try a volley.
- Take a throw in.
- Respect the referee.
- Ignore spectators.
- Do my best.
- Enjoy the game.
- Encourage a team mate.
- Wear my boots (etc).
- Run a kilometre.
- Have a shot (etc).

Key Skills:

- Active listening, to recall what other people say.

Development:

- Lots of variations available, including 'In my kit bag I have…'; 'For breakfast today I had…(it doesn't have to be true!); 'After the game I am going to…'

A third element of developing good teamwork is to encourage players to take responsibility for an aspect of running the club. We have already touched on this in the mental health section of the book, but we can look now in more detail at the kind of roles an inventive coach can create to give their players a sense of responsibility. The list below is not exclusive, and some of the roles will depend on the circumstances of training and playing, but it gives an idea of the range of responsibilities a player can take. If there are too many players for each to have a role, then consider dividing the squad into two or three, and split the roles on a weekly basis.

- Captain (strongly suggest this role is rotated).
- Vice-Captain (ditto above).

- Ambassador: Welcome the opposition to home games.
- Ambassador: Welcome the referee to home games (for example, if there is a club house, showing the referee to their changing room).
- Lights – make sure indoor lights are off at the end of a session.
- Setting up drills – two or three players can be responsible for this but check with parents that they can arrive early.
- Clearing up drills – as above.
- Ball pumper.
- Store shed organiser.
- Kit person – where players arrive in their kit, this person can be responsible for making sure there are some spares – shin pads, socks, shirt, shorts, goalie gloves etc.
- Litter (clearing not leaving…)
- Squad organiser – reminding of matches, times etc.

At the same time, we need to engender in our players the traits of a team player. These are learned and instilled by the example we set, as coaches. Hopefully, our players will arrive with many of the traits already in place, having been set there by their parents, but we know that this is not always the case. Nevertheless, we set the tone at training and at matches, and we will help our team and the individuals within it if we promote the values of the team player.

Each club will have their own slightly different take on this, but we might say a team player is one that:

1. Understands their role within the team. It is the job of the coach to make this clear.
2. Works collaboratively with others. In other words, recognises that the collective is stronger, and more important, than the individual.
3. Is accountable. In other words, they do not blame others for their mistakes. At the same time, they recognise that errors are inevitable in soccer, and use them for growth rather than to beat themselves up.
4. Is flexible and willing to adapt and change.
5. Has a positive attitude.
6. Has empathy towards others. This includes team mates, referees, coaches, spectators and the opposition.
7. Has respect for others. This involves being inclusive, not just passing to mates or always picking the same person to work with them.

Persuade the club chairman to add these traits to the club's paperwork, put them up in the clubhouse, make a mnemonic of the headings, put these characteristics in the club's statement of purpose. Every soccer player knows that the team is stronger than the individual. The younger we can help children to understand this the better for them and their club.

It almost goes without saying that these team work skills will not only help players in their soccer progress, but in their general living. Collaboration is a vital skill for school, for creating friendships, for living with others. Once more, soccer shows how it not only provides an outlet for energy and a source of fun, but also that it makes a vital and often under rated contribution to the all-round development of an individual, especially one who is still learning about their position in the world.

Fun Games

We've looked at some of the more emotional and cognitive elements of child development within the field of soccer in the last two chapters, but it is vital that we do not lose track of the fact that for the players (and the coach) sessions must be fun. So we will finish with some fun based games, each of which help to develop an aspect of the growing soccer player, but do so in an enjoyment filled way.

Drill: Crocker

A fun end of season game, best played when the weather is warm. It is a sort of combination of rounders, cricket and soccer, and coaches can adapt it to suit their own interests and requirements.

Use With: All ages.

Objectives: Score 'runs'.

Equipment: Ball, cones to mark out grid areas, small goals.

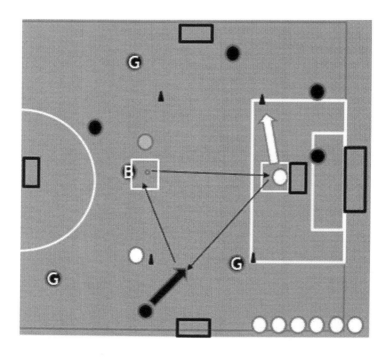

(Note: The white squares mark the 'bowling' grid – the black circle with a 'B' inside is located here – and the 'batting' grid, which has a white circle representing the batter inside.)

Operation of Drill:

Split the group into two teams and each side have a turn at 'batting' and 'fielding'. The game is quite quick so the coach can allow two or three innings. The winners are the side who score most runs. The definition of how to score runs is explained below.

134

Batting:

- Players take turns to move to the 'kicking grid', shown by the white square in front of a small goal in the diagram. Batsmen/kickers defend this small goal by kicking the ball away from it. This is also how they score runs.

- The ball is fed to them (see bullet point under 'Fielding' below) and they must kick it and then run as far around the posts as they can get. The white line represents the direction of running. They aim to complete the square of four cones but may stop at any post (cone) if they feel they will not make it to the next.

- If the 'bowl' is legal and the batsman/kicker misses it, then they must run to the first post only. However, if the ball goes into the goal the batsman/kicker is out.

Fielding:

- Three of the team are 'Goalkeepers'. They wear a hat or bib to identify them. Goalkeepers can change during an innings. Goalkeepers can use any part of their body, including their hands, to play the ball. Note: only the

135

fielding side is allowed goalkeepers, when 'batting', nobody can use their hands.

- One of the team is the bowler. They 'bowl' the ball either by kicking it towards the 'batter', or throwing it underarm, depending on the rules set by the coach. The bowler 'bowls' from a grid marked with cones. (White square in the diagram).
- The remaining fielders can only use the parts of their body permitted in the laws of soccer to play the ball, (ie – not their hands or arms.)

Scoring Runs:

- One run is scored for running past all of the posts but stopping on the way.
- Four runs for clearing the posts in one go.
- Six runs for scoring into one of the goals set around the playing area.
- One run and an extra ball for any delivery from the bowler that is too wide, or too high (above knee height)
- Note: when the ball is returned to the possession of the bowler in their bowling grid, players must stop at the next post they reach.

Getting Out:

A player is OUT if:

- The bowler plays a legal bowl which goes into the goal behind the batsman/kicker.
- A goalkeeper catches a kick before it bounces.
- A fielder hits the post to which a player is running with the ball. (Goalkeepers may use their hands to throw the ball onto the post, or touch the post with it. Other fielders may only 'pass' the ball against the post.)
- Two players end up on the same post after the bowler has controlled the ball in their grid. Both players out.
- The coach might decide that after a certain number of players are out – say half the team – the innings is over.

Key Skills:

- Passing.
- First time shooting.
- Goalkeeping skills.
- Tactical awareness.

Development:

- Allow the bowler more licence to deliver balls.
- Allow strikers up to three chances to run.

Drill: Solf

This is a fun activity for a late season session, or perhaps one to play when there is no game coming up. There is less exercise involved than with most of the drills in this book, so use only when the weather is good. Note a large playing area is needed, and if there are multiple training sessions taking place then some careful communication with fellow coaches is important.

Use With: All ages. Older players probably get more out of the game.

Objectives: Play the ball accurately to hit a target.

Equipment: Balls. Mannequins or large cones to act as the 'hole'; cones etc to use as hazards.

138

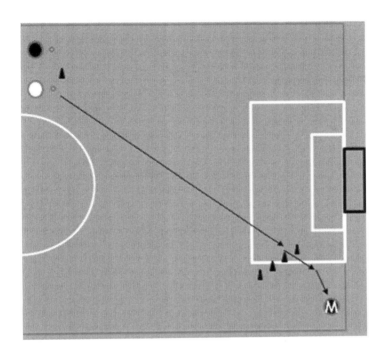

Operation of Drill: Set up six or eight 'holes' as in golf. Have a tee for each hole, marked with a cone, set some hazards, like bunkers made of cones etc, set a mannequin as the hole a good distance from the tee. If space allows, some holes can be shorter – par threes – some longer, par fives.

Divide the players into groups of three or four.

Players 'tee off' with a goalkeeper's kick for distance. Players then use a variety of kicking skills – the drive for distance, the chip to

139

clear an obstacle, a swerve kick to go round an obstacle (for advanced players) and a firm instep pass as a putt to strike the mannequin.

This is a long drill, and can take most of a session to complete.

Key Skills:

- Striking the ball correctly in a number of kicking techniques.

Development:

If time and equipment allows, try setting up a 'Crazy Solf'; eg use small goals with obstructions in front. Skittles (fizzy pop bottles half filled with water work well), one 'hole' where a keeper can save the ball, and the player must play it from where it lands, etc.

Drill: Tag Rugby

This drill is good fun and provides a nice contrast to foot-based sports activities. It can help players with their hand eye coordination and develops teamwork skills and tactical awareness. The coach does not need any knowledge of rugby union, as this is a hugely trimmed down game.

Use With: All ages.

Objectives: Develop speed and team work skills to score tries.

Equipment: Tag belts. If these are unavailable then use touch. Here an opponent must touch the ball carrier with both hands on either side of the hips.

Ball. A rugby shaped ball is ideal, but a small football works. Even a normal size three or four ball is small enough, just, to use.

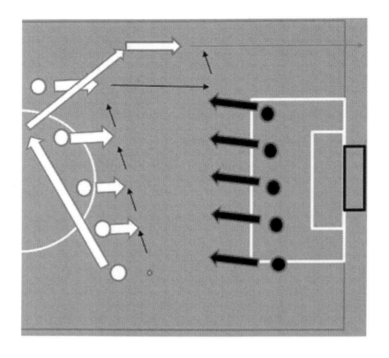

Operation of Drill: There are few rules:

- No conventional tackling. A tackle is either pulling off a tag, or double touching as described above if playing the touch version.
- No forward play: So no scrums, rucks, mauls or line outs. If play stops then this counts as a 'tackle', rugby league style, and play restarts with a free pass to the side in possession. If the ball or player goes out of play, then possession switches to the other side.

- After 6 tackles (eg tag pulled out, or play stops) possession switches. The referee calls the tackle numbers so players know how many plays they have left before losing possession.
- Passes can only be lateral or backwards. (Penalty – possession changes)
- Tries are score by placing the ball over the line.
- Safety note: if playing on a soccer pitch, play either across the pitch or between the edges of the two penalty areas. This reduces the risk of the players running into a goal post.

Key Skills:

- Timing passes.
- Teamwork in defense and attack.

Development:

- Introduce 'conversions'. Use a football. Set a reasonably challenge distance depending on the age range. Team who scored appoint a goalie, who can be anybody except the try scorer. Try scorer must chip or volley from hands the ball from the point set by the coach. If the goalkeeper catches the ball before it bounces, the conversion is complete.

Drill: Do this, Now Do this…

Such a simple game, great fun, and one which works as an original warm up and helps develop individual skills as well. The game is based on the traditional 'Simon says…' format. We've used this well beyond the age range covered by this book, and it works every time…

Use With: All ages.

Objectives: Have some fun while warming up, and also developing active listening.

Equipment: Balls.

Operation of Drill: Each player has a ball. The coach issues an instruction. The players follow the instruction, but only if it is prefaced with 'Now…' If it is not, they continue with the previous instruction. For example:

1. **Now** dribble the ball (players dribble)

144

2. **Now** dribble left (players dribble left)

3. Pass to someone else (players continue to dribble left because the instruction did not begin with 'Now...' Any player who made a mistake collects their ball and waits until the everybody is out. This doesn't usually take more than thirty seconds)

4. **Now** pass the ball (they do)

5. **Now** stand on the ball with alternate feet (players put one foot then the other on top of the ball)

6. Touch the ball with your hand (they continue to stand on the ball, anyone who moves to touch the ball is out)

7. TIP: When it gets down to the last few, do two or three 'false' instructions in a row. This usually ends the game quickly!

Key Skills:

- Active listening.
- Individual skills.

Development:

The game works as a physical exercise without a ball. Players stand in front of the coach well spread out. The coach makes a movement, for example, lifts an arm, or runs on the spot. If he or she says 'Do this...' the players copy, if the coach says 'Do that...' they do not. This is a harder and faster version of the game.

Drill: Multi Goals

Organised chaos. Without the organised bit. But huge fun. This game is full of action, but at the same time requires tactical thinking, teamwork and soccer skills.

Use With: All ages.

Objectives: Score more goals than your opponents, utilising soccer skills and employing effective tactics.

Equipment: Eight small goals. Two super soft balls, or sponge balls (for safety as players will not necessarily be facing play.)

146

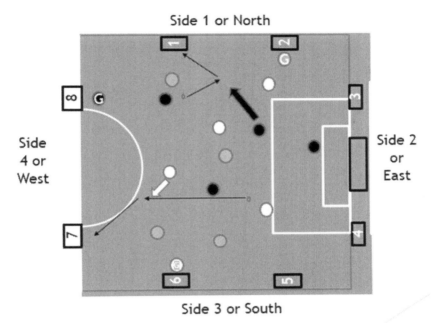

Side 1 or North

Side 4 or West

Side 2 or East

Side 3 or South

Operation of Drill: Three teams of five or six. One goalkeeper who cannot score, and the remainder outfield players who can. Square pitch (around half a normal pitch) with two small goals on each side. Label each side, eg 1, 2, 3 and 4, or North, East, South and West. Two balls.

1. The three goalkeepers each chose one goal. The goals must be on different sides of the pitch.
2. Play begins with two goalkeepers.
3. If, for example, the WHITE goalie is on SIDE ONE – their side now try to score in either of the goals on SIDE

TWO. Meanwhile, if the GREY 'keeper is on SIDE TWO, the greys try to score in one of the goals on SIDE THREE. And so on.

4. The BLACK team must try to win a ball.

5. Once, for example, WHITES score in one of the goals on SIDE TWO, their next target is to score in side three.

6. Normal rules of soccer apply whilst the ball is in play, except there are two balls and three teams.

7. Goalkeepers may move to any side where there is no goalkeeper. They can do so at any time. They can switch between the goals on that side as they wish.

8. After a goal is scored, if there is a goalkeeper on that side, then this player restarts. If there is not, then the team that scored restart. (Clearly an advantage.)

9. Play for no more than five minutes.

10. Good luck to the coach in keeping score.

Key Skills:

• Communication with team mates.

• Tactical awareness – seeing how the game is developing.

• Making wise tactical decisions regarding whether to defend or attack. Or both.

148

Development:

- The game works with one ball, although is a little less fun. If no soft balls are available, then use a normal ball in this variation.

Drill: Skittle Alley

Building on the development suggestion for Crazy Solf, this is a fun game which encourages players to keep the ball on the ground whilst trying out different kicking techniques to knock down 'Skittles'. It is possible to buy large, soft skittles (cones do not work, they are too stable to knock over easily) but two litre fizzy drink bottles half filled with water to give some stability work well. Collect plenty over a few weeks, getting players to bring them to sessions. (Collecting them with the water already added saves a lot of fiddly time!)

Use With: Any age.

Objectives: Strike the ball with accuracy using a mixture of spin and power as the situation dictates.

149

Equipment: Lots of 'skittles'. Lots of balls.

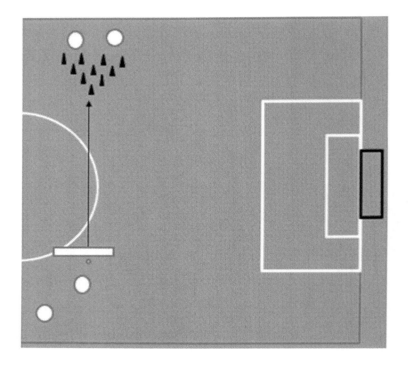

(Note: in this diagram the 'cones' represent skittles, and the thick white line is the marker behind which the shot must be played. Set up two or three alleys to keep involvement high.)

Operation of Drill: Set up ten skittles like a ten pin bowling alley. Place a cone or line as the point to play the pass/shot. This will depend on the age and ability of the players. Ten to twenty metres is a good distance. Players have two or three shots (two is best, to keep players involved, if

150

ability allows.) They must knock down as many skittles as possible in their turn. Operate as in ten pin bowling with strikes and spares and keep track of scoring. Encourage players to wait by the pins when it is not their go. Then they can reset the skittles before the next player and return balls.

Key Skills:

- Striking the ball in a variety of ways along the ground:
  - o Use the laces to drive the ball for power – will knock down more skittles, but is harder to keep on the ground and maintain accuracy;
  - o Use the instep for accuracy to knock down one or two pins left standing;
  - o Use the outside of the foot to impart spin when needing the ball to deflect onto a second skittle (very hard skill!!)

Development:

- Add a 'barrier' on certain round, over which players must chip the ball to reach the skittles.

We have offered drills, tips and activities to use with our eight to twelve year old kids. These can form the basis of a season's training regime, one which will help our players to develop their soccer skills whilst ensuring sessions are productive and, most importantly, fun.

Conclusion

Coaching children of this age is a great job. It does require dedication, planning, a positive outlook and a lot of patience, but it is also hugely rewarding.

Experienced coaches will hopefully take some of the drills and ideas presented in this book and use them, or adapt them, to provide variety in their sessions. Or to address a specific training needs their players have. Newer coaches might also take guidance from the philosophy behind the theories presented here.

If we could sum up coaching eight to twelve year old kids in just a few bullet points, they would be as follows:

1. Plan carefully.
2. Be flexible.
3. Place safety at the forefront of every session and match, but close behind this comes fun.
4. Be positive. Because your players certainly will be.
5. Get to know your players as well as you can.
6. Enjoy yourself.

We should never lose sight of the good we are doing as coaches. We are taking young people, the most important members of our society, and we are giving them an outlet for their energy, a chance to really enjoy themselves, an opportunity to learn about a game they love, a capability to stay physically and emotionally fit, the opening to make new friends, develop confidence, achieve resilience and mental strength and become the best adults they can be.

That's an impressive list of achievements and something about which every one of us should be proud.

The end… almost!

Reviews are not easy to come by.

As an independent author with a tiny marketing budget, I rely on readers, like you, to leave a short review on Amazon.

Even if it's just a sentence or two!

So if you enjoyed the book, please browse to the product page and leave a review as shown below:

I am very appreciative for your review as it truly makes a difference.

Thank you from the bottom of my heart for purchasing this book and reading it to the end.

Made in the USA
Las Vegas, NV
08 December 2024

13635804R00087